# Raising
# Cooperative Kids

# Praise for *Raising Cooperative Kids*

"An excellent book that brings the best of longstanding, proven, and highly effective parenting practices to the modern age. This book is a must for every parent and every professional who works with children."
—Jeffrey Bernstein, PhD, author of *10 Days to a Less Defiant Child*

"This is a wonderful book with clear, easy-to-apply, and workable techniques based on both clinical experience and research. From defining and setting goals to the critical importance of family play, *Raising Cooperative Kids* provides a concise and practical blueprint for parents who want to enjoy their kids." —Thomas W. Phelan, PhD, author of *1-2-3 Magic: Effective Discipline for Children 2–12*

"This book is a special gift to accomplish one of the hardest and most rewarding jobs we will face in our lifetime: raising children. Marion and Jerry share their years of experience studying human behavior and give simple, yet powerful, tools to help parents. You will see yourself in some of the chapters, sometimes doing the right thing, sometimes doing the wrong thing. Enjoy the gift, have fun practicing and take comfort that you're doing the best you can." —Jim Wotring, senior deputy director, Department of Behavioral Health, Washington, DC

"Marion and Jerry are the foremost experts on parenting in the world and their research, writing, and professional work have helped millions of families. The information in this book is based on rigorous scientific study. As a parent, I trusted these principles in raising my own children. As a professor and clinician, I spread the word to clinicians in training in their work with families. If you are going to rely on one book to secure a better future for your children, this is the book to use." —Thomas J. Dishion, PhD, professor in the Department of Psychology, Arizona State University, founder of "The Family Check-Up," and author of *Preventive Parenting with Love, Encouragement, and Limits: The Preschool Years*

# Raising
# Cooperative Kids

---

## Proven Practices for a
## Connected, Happy Family

---

Marion S. Forgatch, PhD, Gerald R. Patterson, PhD,
and Tim Friend

Conari Press

This edition first published in 2017
by Conari Press, an imprint of
Red Wheel/Weiser, LLC
With offices at:
65 Parker Street, Suite 7
Newburyport, MA 01950
*www.redwheelweiser.com*

ISBN: 978-1-57324-690-3
Library of Congress Cataloging-in-Publication Data available upon request

Cover design by Jim Warner
Cover photograph © Cultura Limited / Superstock
Typeset in Adobe Caslon

MAR
Printed in Canada

10  9  8  7  6  5  4  3  2  1

*To families everywhere.*
*We honor your dreams and struggles.*

# Contents

# Cooperation Makes It Happen

---

O ne of the greatest gifts parents can bestow on their children is a happy childhood. As family research psychologists with our own blended family of five grown-up children, Jerry and I have shared a lifelong passion to understand what a "happy childhood" means and what it takes to raise "well-adjusted" children. The simple answer is—good parenting. But what is that?

After studying the good, the bad, and the ugly in relationships between thousands of parents and their children, we have found that the most important factor successful families have in common is a spirit of cooperation. The parenting techniques we have developed instill cooperation in children; they tap deep-rooted human instincts that are universal across cultural and economic lines. Whether you are rich, or poor, or middle-class; whether you live on a farm, in the suburbs, or in the city; whether you are black, brown, or white—the cooperative spirit is the same.

Our research reveals that cooperation is the keystone that makes the essential building blocks of children's behavior fall into place. Our parenting techniques, embraced so far by thousands of families, enable parents to teach their children new behaviors while promoting a home environment with few family conflicts. Cooperation, which parents must teach to their children, is the foundation of healthy child development.

Now, you may wonder: What do we mean by "cooperative children?"

Cooperative children pay attention; they follow rules, and work and play well with others. With siblings and peers, they share, take turns, and are good sports whether they win or lose. With adults—parents, teachers, and coaches—cooperative children *willingly* follow directions. Willingness is an essential distinction here. It's one thing when children behave out of fear of being punished. It's quite another when they *want* to follow your directions and get along with others rather than argue, refuse, and create conflicts. Cooperation, which most children are eager to learn, opens new dimensions of family life. It's the secret sauce that makes parenting a joy.

Cooperative children enjoy pleasing others without being so-called people pleasers. Following directions seems to come naturally to them most of the time. That cooperative spirit then generates harmonious teamwork that spreads throughout the family. We have conducted studies to learn what parents do to promote cooperation in their children. This book shares what we have learned from our research.

That research began about fifty years ago when Jerry read studies reporting that the traditional talk and play therapies he had so carefully learned to use did not change children's behavior. The traditional approach was to work directly with children while their parents sat patiently in the waiting room hoping that magic would take place. After these sessions, parents brought their children home knowing little about what had just transpired and knowing even less about what to do to follow up. Jerry decided to try something new.

A scientist to his core, Jerry began by watching how parents and children behave with each other. He visited the homes of families with well-adjusted children and families struggling with behavior problems. He sat quietly in the corners of their homes, observing their everyday lives, writing down what the parents did and how the children reacted, and how the parents reacted in turn. He wanted to understand why some children are cooperative and well-behaved while others are antagonistic and get into trouble. And he wanted to know the role that parents play in that interaction. I joined him in his studies in the 1970s, and together we have developed and tested a set of parenting techniques that help families change. We have seen that the parenting practices we describe in this book promote children's cooperation. In turn, that helps them get along better with siblings at home, follow parents' directions, learn routines and new behaviors, and do well in school and out in the community. Parents benefit by being less stressed and happier in their relationships at home and at work. A landmark study of single mothers who used our techniques found that they even became more successful financially.

This book draws from our decades of research into what parents can do to make things better—and what factors make things worse. We have formulated our parenting practices into simple strategies that are easy to follow. Each chapter presents at least one such strategy, and we have provided a list of them at the end of the book so you can easily refer to them. Make sure, as you apply them, that you include all the elements and follow them in the suggested sequence. Properly applied, these strategies promote a cooperative spirit in children.

## Our Methods

To make sure that our strategies work, we tested them using what is called randomized controlled trials. That is the same rigorous approach the medical profession uses to determine whether or not a drug or procedure is effective. In our trials, we randomly assigned some parents to receive our techniques while others were assigned to receive treatment as usual or no treatment. We tested families before and after the intervention period, and for follow-up periods from months to years. Then we compared the outcomes for the different randomized groups. This is the way to be objective and discover whether a treatment or technique works. You can learn about our studies at www.isii.net or at www.oslc.org.

The success of our evidence-based parenting methods has attracted attention worldwide. With demand for our parenting approach increasing rapidly, I established Implementation Sciences International, Inc. (ISII) in 2001 to separate the ongoing research at our research center, called the Oregon Social Learning Center (OSLC), from the tasks of training practitioners in our methods, writing manuals for practitioners and parents, and handling the logistics for launching our ever-growing programs. Today, demand is greater than we can meet, so we decided to write this book to make our techniques available to as many parents as possible.

Because we have carefully tested our methods and subjected our findings to independent review by other scientists, you can be confident that they work. Our group at OSLC has published more than 1,000 papers in peer-reviewed professional journals and contributed dozens of chapters in academic books. Jerry's published work on "coercion theory" and parenting has been cited more than 50,000 times by other scientists. The fields of psychology, sociology, and criminology have adopted Jerry's coercion theory as an underlying explanation for children's behavior problems.

Studies show that the parenting strategies we recommend are successful in promoting children's healthy adjustment and preventing problems from developing. The same techniques also reduce or eliminate problems that are already present.

We wrote this book to share what we have learned so you can create the family you will love to love. This book is a journey we take together. Be sure to follow our road map through each chapter and don't jump ahead. The ground you cover in one chapter sets you up to find your way through the next. You will enhance your success at building new skills if you do the exercises in the order presented, chapter by chapter. Each exercise builds on the previous one; in the end, all the skills link together to create strong, confident parents.

Each chapter ends with a practice assignment that gives you the opportunity to try our strategies and adjust them to fit your values and goals as parents, as well as your children's temperament, age, developmental stage, personal interests, and talents. In some chapters, we have added a section called *What Do Parents Say?* That section provides comments made by real parents—some praising the parenting strategies, others raising questions about how to use them.

Family living is often like an intricate dance in which family members learn to move in synchrony with each other. We describe this complicated choreography, then use family scenarios to help you tailor our strategies to the needs of you and your children. Because all families get out of synch and sometimes step on each other's toes, we show families experiencing problems based on actual circumstances we have observed (and experienced ourselves) over the years. Then we "rewind" the situation and play out the scenario again, following the techniques introduced in that chapter.

Because today's families are so diverse, we describe different family structures (two-parent, single-parent, and blended families) with children of differing ages and genders. As you read the scenarios, try to imagine your family in the situation. After you have tried out a strategy, you can adjust it to suit your family members' individual needs and circumstances. For example, the kinds of praise you use to encourage your two-year-old will differ from the way you praise your twelve-year-old.

While our techniques are appropriate for children of all ages, this book will be most helpful for parents of children from toddlerhood through the tween years, when children are most open to learning from you. You will probably need some additional approaches to address the issues that arise during the teen years. Our books *Parents and Adolescents, Living Together, Part 1* and *Part 2* (Patterson & Forgatch; Forgatch & Patterson) are good resources for this.

## Shining the Light

We start in the first chapter by explaining why children say "no." Then we help you define your goals as parents—think of it as your parenting wish list. Creating goals and making a plan to achieve them is a skill you will find useful time and time again as you raise your children. We show you how to determine the goals you set for your children and how to encourage progress toward those goals. As your children's best teachers, you set them up for success and then reward their many small achievements. We call this *shining the light on the behavior you want to grow*. Our strategies will help you balance positive reinforcement with negative sanctions in a way that leads to cooperation.

When teaching children how to thrive in today's society, you have to give them room to make mistakes. Your children *will* make mistakes. So will you. They don't have to be perfect, and neither do you. As a general rule, well-adjusted young children, whether they live in primitive rural villages or upscale suburban neighborhoods, comply with their parents' directives about 70 percent of the time. As children get older, their compliance rises to more than 80 percent. We use these figures as a benchmark for successful parenting. Knowing that children (and parents) don't have to be perfect allows you to concentrate on what they (and you) do right.

Changing unwanted behaviors that are already established is tougher than teaching new behaviors. That's normal. In fact, changing entrenched behavior is one of the most challenging things we do as human beings. How many times have you made New Years' resolutions only to find yourself slipping back into the habits you wanted to break? So, we ask you to remember that, sometimes, the positive steps you and your children take are so small that you can overlook them and allow mistakes to overshadow them. We will show you how to break goals into small steps and, as part of teaching through encouragement, how to "catch" your children being good.

As we all know, parenting involves a lot of trial and error. We have spent our careers studying the many challenges of raising children so that we can help you avoid common errors and adopt parenting techniques that have been proven to work. You can finally stop wasting time on hindsight and its latent 20/20 vision. We offer foresight that will allow you to create a vision for the family you want. You have the vision and we have strategies to encourage the positive behaviors that are shared by happy children and functional families throughout the world.

Our parenting approach prevents behavior problems from arising and improves stability in families, including those undergoing stressful changes like divorce, relocation, starting in a new school, or adjusting to a new step-family. Recently, we published a prevention study in which we followed the progress of single mothers for nine years after they participated in our parenting program. The results were exciting. After intervention, the lives of the mothers and their children continued to improve dramatically: mothers' parenting practices improved; their depression levels dropped; their children's cooperation improved and behavior problems often vanished; mothers obtained better jobs and achieved higher incomes; and most important, families were happier and more functional compared to those that did not receive the training. In another of our studies with step-families, we found that parents who used our techniques increased cooperation within the family, reduced children's aggressive behaviors, relieved problems at home and school, and built happier marriages.

## Practice, Practice, Practice

In the pages that follow, we address social skills, tantrums, discipline, chores, routines, communication with children and partners, connecting with teachers, ensuring children's safety, sticking together as parents when the kids pit you against each other, and having fun as a family. One of the most effective ways to transform our strategies from words on a page into new skills is to practice them with a spouse, partner, or friend before you try them with your children. Choose a specific family situation you are experiencing—anything from not doing chores to arguing with you and other adults. Then focus on one parenting tool at a time in the order we've presented them.

Play the role of parent while your partner plays the child. Play out the scenario as it takes place in the worst of times—for example, as you have seen it happen in other families. Consider exaggerating. Most families enjoy some good laughs from this exercise. Take turns playing different roles so both you and your partner have a chance to see the experience through the eyes of your children. Then try the role play again using the strategies presented in the chapters. This approach of doing it not so well and then using new tools works much like the rewind scenarios we give throughout the book.

Role play dramatizes the power of the techniques and makes it easier for you to see what a difference they can make. Feeling shy about role playing is normal. But parents tell us how enlightening it is when they use this approach. Role play allows you to practice the techniques before using them with your children. Parents say that the better they become at applying our strategies, the more they feel as if they have gained superpowers. If you take the time to role play, our techniques will come to life for you as you move through the chapters.

Each new skill presented here adds to a repertoire that you can use for increasingly complex situations and behaviors for your children. Because the skills are practical, they are easy to learn. Nothing that follows on these pages is based on opinion (we all have them) or on the parenting "fad *du jour*." You will not hear about helicopter parents, indigo children, detachment parenting, or Training Up. What you will read is as close to a commonsense parenting manual as you will find.

By the time you finish this book, you will be using these skills automatically. When you need to refresh your understanding of a specific technique, refer to the list of strategies and resources at the back of the book. Whether you are just starting your family or are well underway, the present behavior of your children is the best predictor of their future behavior. So, if you want to make changes, now is the time to begin.

*Chapter One*

# Imagine

---

As parents, we shape our children's behavior from the day they are born. Their behaviors—desirable and undesirable alike—become established as we reinforce them through our own actions, reactions, and inactions. In this chapter, we'll discuss how you can encourage cooperation in your children and help you to become aware of behaviors that may innocently send the wrong messages.

As Jerry studied families in their homes, he developed what has become known as "coercion theory." Coercion starts out as a vital, natural survival instinct that can be found in infants as well as baby birds. Before children develop language, they communicate their needs to be fed, held, or have their diapers changed by crying. Unattended infants can fly into little fits of apparent rage. It's their only way of telling you that they need something, and they need it *now*. As they begin to develop language, we have to teach children to ask for what they need. If we don't, that coercive behavior can allow toddlers to control their parents. To see unadulterated coercion in action, watch a three-year-old throw a temper tantrum in a grocery store. See how the parent and child react to each other. Observe the escalation in the intensity of emotions during the exchange. This is a battle of wills between a little kid and a grown-up. Watch how it ends, who wins, and why.

Coercion lies at the root of most of the battles we see between siblings and between parents and children. You can think of coercion as a dark side of human nature inside all of us. Understanding what coercion is and how it interferes with loving relationships can enable you to recognize it when it arises and do something about it. Because coercion is the cause of so much of the trouble between parents and young children, reducing it is a core component of our parenting techniques. When parents learn to reduce coercive actions in their children—and in themselves—cooperative behaviors have a better chance to grow and thrive. When we first become parents, many of us start out with vague dreams for ourselves, our individual children, and our families as a whole. You have probably had some kind of vision of the family you wanted ever since you were a child—though it is rare for anyone to sit down with us when we are young (and most receptive) and explain how to raise a happy family, let alone model how it is done. Your vision, however amorphous it may be, was likely influenced by the strengths and values that determined how you were raised—for better or worse.

Sit back and imagine the family you want. What you imagine is probably different from your partner's ideal family. If one of you had a great childhood, you will surely follow in the footsteps of those amazing parents. If your childhood was rocky, you may be thinking of different ways to raise your children. Unfortunately, many of us are so busy that we don't spend much time planning our parenting strategies. We live in a different world from the one in which we grew up. Raising children is more expensive than ever, employers demand more work, our relationships become loaded with stress, and we sacrifice our dreams to focus on the problems at hand. Now is the time to rekindle your dreams and get ready to create the changes you want for your family. Changing bad habits and teaching new skills require that you think carefully about your goals. We urge you to think big and reach high to create the family you have always wanted.

Dreams can lie dormant and may even die unless you awaken them and imagine ways to make them come true. Once you conceive your dreams, how do you give birth to them? It's easy to say: "I want my children to get along with others or do well in school." It is quite another thing to say: "Here's how I will make it happen." You start by setting goals. Begin with something feasible, and then break down the goal into steps using the Goldilocks rule—not too big, not too small, but just right. When you accomplish one goal, set a new one.

For instance, imagine teaching your children to get ready for bed on their own. Our approach is to first show them each tiny step; then we patiently teach them to put the steps together—take a bath, dress for bed, and brush their teeth. Gradually, your children learn to do it all themselves, and you can move on to another set of skills. Setting goals and planning the steps required to reach them is a kind of telescoping process—you look ahead to the future, you zoom back to the present, and you figure out how to get from here to that distant place. With practice, your skill at making long- and short-term goal statements will grow, and you will become a master of making dreams come true.

## Setting Goals

The first tool for turning your family dreams into actions is a goal statement, one of the most basic instruments in your family-management toolkit. Goals are less abstract and more realistic than dreams. They enable you to design action plans to accomplish your family objectives.

Goal statements that work have certain universal qualities: they are realistic, yet they reach beyond wherever you are at the moment; they are future-oriented; they state what you want (not what you don't want); and they are framed positively. After working with parents and studying families for years, we can say with confidence that achieving a goal is easier if you first identify what you want. Once you define a goal, you open new pathways for you and your children to follow. Your journey will be most satisfying when you base your course on your family's individual values and resources. You are in charge of your family—no one else. Your dreams are whatever *you* want them to be. Here are the basic elements of a goal statement that will set you on the path to achieving your dreams.

## Strategies for Successful Goal Statements

- ✏ Be specific.

- ✏ Frame your goal positively.

- ✏ State what you want.

- ✏ Be future-oriented.

- ✏ Choose a goal that can be broken into small steps.

- ✏ State the goal so a stranger can understand it.

Think of two families who are about to travel across the country from coast to coast. Both families live in the same town on the East Coast and are traveling to the same area on the West Coast. Since each journey begins and ends at the same place, you could say that they have the same goal—to travel from point A to point B. But for each family, the goals of the trip depend on a number of factors—available time and resources, personal interests, and family strengths. Considering these factors, each family checks various routes and makes a plan.

The Hancock family has two weeks to make a round trip across country to attend a family reunion celebrating the grandparents' fiftieth anniversary. As much as they wish to fly to save time—like some of their in-laws—they can't afford airline tickets for the two adults, three children, and beagle that make up their family. However, they have a perfectly fine minivan that can deliver them safely to their destination and back. If they stick to the interstates and mom and dad take turns driving on the way out, they can take it easy coming home and do a little sight-seeing.

The Rodriguez family has a full month to spend with an RV fitted for camping. Their final destination is the husband's parents' house on the West Coast. The purpose of their trip is vacation. Time is not a factor. Their goal is to see the country and visit points of interest to them along the way, like the world's largest ball of string and Yellowstone's geysers.

These two families design entirely different trips, even though their start and end points are the same. The Hancocks' route is straightforward, emphasizing speed and efficiency. The Rodriguez family plots a winding course following blue-line roads that avoid busy interstates and take them to beautiful lakes, national parks, and points of historical interest. As you can see, goals incorporate something more than simple outcomes. Individual family values and practical conditions are critical factors that capture the components of dreams. As each family designs its travel plan, they begin by defining a destination.

## Long-Term and Short-Term Goals

Long-term goals can feel like impossible dreams, especially if you have to travel far to reach them. Yet, goals serve as magnets that draw you forward. Since every journey begins with a single step, make the first steps in your goal statement easy to achieve, and then enjoy a bit of success. One of your goals is probably to raise happy, well-adjusted, and cooperative children—after all, you're reading this book. But that may seem like a tall order.

When formulating your goal statements, begin by making two lists—one for your long-term dreams for your children and one for more immediate goals, things that can happen today or this week. For the long-term goals, think big. Be ambitious. Most parents say they want their children to be happy, healthy, resilient, self-disciplined, skillful, independent, and cooperative. This list describes general qualities that reflect your values, which are like points on a compass that draw you in certain directions. Next make a list of the small steps needed to achieve your long-term goals. As parents, we can influence long-term outcomes for our families, but to do that, we have to take little actions day by day. Life is a process of ongoing change that you control when you convert goals into tiny steps.

Parents' lists of short-term goals tend to include daily behaviors like doing chores independently, following rules, being respectful, and cooperating with directions. These short-term lists involve behaviors that form habits. When habits are appropriate, they lead to well-being. Moreover, your children's well-being depends a lot on your own habits. We all have good habits and bad habits. Once we have families, we need to think about how our habits influence our children's behavior.

Now, make another list that focuses on your strengths as a person and as a parent. Then make one of your children's strengths, taking into account their unique qualities. Many parents find making a list of their own strengths challenging. If you have trouble with this, think about times when you felt good about something you accomplished, or something your children did that made you feel proud, and take ownership of your contribution.

When the challenges of raising a family seem overwhelming—and maybe not even worth the extraordinary effort—pull out your list of personal strengths and review it. Some of the strengths parents have identified for themselves include patience, warmth, honesty, perseverence, commitment, and fairness. When you are disappointed in the mistakes and choices your children make, take a look at the list you made of their strengths. Parents have identified some of these qualities as honesty, kindness, devotion, humor, adventurousness, and persistence. Once you make your lists, keep them in a safe place and add to them whenever you feel good or something special happens.

When we think about change, we often focus on what is wrong—what needs fixing. This is easier than noticing what you and children do right. Some of the most common complaints we hear from parents about their children's behavior include stubbornness, unwillingness to accept "no" for an answer, whining, arguing, temper tantrums, noncompliance, bedtime problems, bad attitude, procrastination, disrespect, carelessness, thoughtlessness, self-centeredness, and fear of trying new things. Review the elements of a successful goal statement as you turn these problem behaviors into active goal statements. Remember that a goal statement says what you want so clearly that a stranger will understand what you mean: it is future-oriented and positively framed, and it can be broken down into small steps. Goal statements have the same basic ingredients whether you want to raise cooperative children, read a novel by Isabel Allende in Spanish, lose weight, or catch a trout.

Let's apply these ingredients to several common behavioral problems.

| ☹ Problem Behaviors | ☺ Goal Behaviors |
|---|---|
| Whining | Talking like a big boy/girl |
| Noncompliance | Compliance |
| Stubbornness | Cooperation, compliance |
| Temper tantrums | Accepting "no," compliance |
| Bedtime problems | Getting to bed on time |
| Bad attitude | Cheerfulness, cooperation |
| Procrastination | Starting on time |
| Shouting inside | Using inside voice |
| Thoughtlessness | Kindness to others, empathy |
| Fear of trying new things | Adventurousness, confidence |
| Won't accept "no" | Accepting "no," cooperation |
| Selfishness | Sharing, generosity |
| Disrespect | Respect |

Notice how often the positive opposite for a problem behavior is compliance or cooperation. For most parents, complaints boil down to the fact that their kids just don't follow directions—at least not without an argument. Some parents say their children use a disrespectful tone of voice when talking to them, or roll their eyes, or. . . you name it. These are not cooperative behaviors.

The building blocks for attaining goals like resilience, independence, self-discipline, and happiness all tend to be based on cooperation. Cooperation involves working together with a spirit of collaboration or teamwork. Cooperative people are pleasant to be around. They are helpful and kind. Parents everywhere say they want their children to follow directions pleasantly, play by the rules, and get along with others, especially family members. When family members cooperate with each other, they enjoy each other's company. The question is how do you bring this about?

## Modeling and Shaping Behavior

Let's take an item on one parent's wish list. A mother wants her three-year-old to stop grabbing for things and instead politely ask to share. She starts by showing her how to do it using several small steps.

Mom (cuddling a teddy bear): Let's pretend we're playing and you want me to share Teddy with you. Remember how to ask to share, sweetheart?

Jill: Gimme Teddy?

Mom: That's right. You ask. And do you remember the magic word?

Jill: Please gimme Teddy?

Mom (giving her the teddy): Much better. Now I'm going to ask you to share. Jill, may I have Teddy back now please?

Jill: But I just got her.

Mom (smiling reassuringly): We're just practicing, honey. May I have Teddy now, please? (pleasantly waiting)

Jill: Okay. Can I have her back?

Mom: Sure. Remember how to ask?

Jill: Can I have Teddy back . . . please?

Mom (clapping): You've got it!

———————

This is an example of modeling and shaping sharing behavior, almost as you would shape a block of clay. Mom started with the raw material and, through a series of small steps, she showed Jill how to behave. She did not require perfection. Although Jill's "Please gimme Teddy" wasn't the height of politeness, it was better than her first demand. Rather than correcting her, Mom praised her for adding the "please" and then modeled a slightly improved version. When Jill complained, Mom simply reminded her they were practicing and restated her request to share. Practice and patience allow you to teach your children the many things they have to learn on the road to growing up. Very few three-year-olds will suddenly begin sharing without guidance, thanks to the more hard-wired coercive nature we discussed earlier.

Take a look at your list of short-term goals and pick one that you would like to start working on in the coming weeks. Be hopeful, yet realistic. For openers, start with a goal that will build on strengths your children already possess. So, if you want one of your children to become more responsible, consider ways in which that child already demonstrates responsibility—perhaps remembering to feed and water the dog regularly. Can you think of things that prompt that behavior consistently? Does the dog give cues? Is there a routine around caring for the dog before breakfast and dinner? Now think of something you'd like done better—something the child already does sometimes, but not reliably. Is there a way to incorporate cues that can help? Or can you help by building in a routine? This is one way you can use your children's existing strengths to add new responsibilities to their repertoire.

Goal statements should be simultaneously ambitious and realistic. They should reach slightly beyond wherever your child is right now. When you teach responsibility, you have to break that goal into steps.

Teach your child to be successful in one arena and then generalize it to another—and another—and another. One step at a time; one goal at a time. As your simple goals are accomplished, you can design goal statements for steps further along in the process of achieving your long-term goal. Eventually, responsibility will become second nature and help guide most of your children's behaviors.

The problem for many parents is that they wait until they are near desperation before seeking help. Then they want a quick solution. As you know, there are no simple fixes for the complexities of raising children. A counselor who barely knows you or your family cannot and *should not* tell you what to do. He or she can only introduce you to tools (hopefully ones that work) and show you how to apply them. As parents, you are the architects. You are in charge of designing your life according to your personal values. You'll be successful if you build on the strengths you and your family already have and plan how to achieve your goals.

## Compromise

Let's look at how one mom used goal statements to overcome a problem in her family. Notice how she had to think about what she wanted and then create steps to get there.

 Lisa and Adam have been married for eight years. They have a seven-year-old daughter, Hanna, and a five-year-old son, Ethan. Saturday mornings are reserved for grocery shopping, running errands, and maintaining the house and yard. Lisa takes errand duty with the kids in tow while Adam cleans the gutters, changes lightbulbs, and fixes whatever needs fixing. Saturday mornings are usually hectic and tensions run high— for Lisa. Grocery shopping is like running a gauntlet. Every aisle is booby-trapped with something to catch the children's attention. She can't get a loaf of bread without an argument: "No, you can't have that.""That's not on mommy's list.""Hanna, put that down." "Ethan, stop throwing mommy's groceries out of the cart." "Hanna, I won't say it again." "Ethan, if you want to ride in the cart, stop sliding out of the seat." Lisa simmers and thinks about how Adam is at home probably chatting with the neighbor about power tools or working in the garage. Lisa decides something has to change.

When she returns home, she sees Adam hooking up a TV set on the wall above his workbench. After helping the kids out of the car, she stares incredulously at Adam and then takes the kids inside for a snack. She returns to the garage, switching her gaze from her husband to the TV and back again: "Are you kidding me?"

Adam smiles, guilt oozing from his pores, and tries to explain: "This was a heck of a deal, honey. Yard sale down the street this morning. Only twenty-five dollars."

Keeping her voice down, Lisa says: "Yes. I'm sure having a TV in the garage is exactly what you need. However, for me, I've had it with this Saturday morning routine where I run all over town doing the shopping with two kids while you pretend to tinker out here. Did I fall into a time warp? Is this the 1950s?"

Adam is taken off guard. He is proud of how he kept up the yard and house maintenance and how neatly he arranged his many tools—most of which he rarely used. He thought they were happy with the way they did things. His wife's anger is a shock that seems to come out of nowhere. He starts to defend himself, but Lisa continues: "Adam, I don't actually think you are a chauvinist. I think you are simply insensitive and selfish, and you have worked it out brilliantly so that you don't have to deal with the kids."

"What do you want?" Adam asks cautiously. Unwittingly, Adam has asked the perfect question.

"I'll tell you what I want. I want Saturday mornings to be easier for me. Let's change places. From now on, you do the grocery shopping with the kids, and I'll stay here and watch TV in the garage."

Lisa storms back through the kitchen. "Daddy will clean up after you when you're done. Mommy has to take a long nap."

Lisa leaves Adam and the kids in the kitchen, shuts the door to the bedroom, and locks it. The day doesn't get any better.

• • •

This situation suggests that Lisa and Adam have more than one or two problems to solve. They've fallen into a pattern that worked well in the past, but it has lost its purpose, especially for Lisa. Some of the problems may feel familiar to you. They certainly are common for most families. And it's particularly difficult if you have to manage the many stressors of daily life on your weekend off from work, times when people need to enjoy each other's company.

Let's label some of the problems in this situation, keeping in mind that, so far, we only have the story from Lisa's perspective. The problems include: grocery shopping, kids' behavior in the store and car (arguing, noncompliance, teasing), and communication between partners. Take a moment and turn those problem behaviors into goal statements, remembering the essential elements required for success: the goal should be future-oriented, state what is desired, be positively framed, and be specific enough for a stranger to understand. Now let's look at ways to break Lisa's goal into smaller steps.

☑ *Grocery shopping* is not a specific statement. It's not really clear whether grocery shopping *per se* is the problem, or if it is shopping with the kids along for the ride. Turning this problem into a clearly defined goal will need more conversation with Lisa.

☑ *Kids' behavior in the grocery store and car.* You probably found this one easier to turn into a goal that comprises several smaller steps, like accepting "no" and following directions. Those are specific actions and parents can tell whether or not they are happening. The underlying goal is for the kids to cooperate with Mom and with each other.

☑ *Communicating with your partner.* It seems pretty clear that Lisa has been harboring bad feelings about this situation for a while. Perhaps this Saturday was worse than others, but her return home did not occasion a collaborative problem-solving discussion with her husband about how to make things better. What would a reasonable goal statement be for this situation? There are many options, and they will reflect your particular values and the strengths in your partnership. Timing is important. Let's say that this couple gets along well when they have a dinner date. Then, they enjoy talking about the children, things at home and in their lives, and their hopes and plans for the future. This is the proper setting for discussions about changing things up—not when Lisa pulled up in the driveway.

If Lisa were to write down a goal statement, what do you imagine she would say? After thinking it through, Lisa decides she likes doing the shopping because she's the one planning meals for the family. She enjoys cooking and she has the time for it because she gets home from work at least two hours before Adam. The problem is the kids. Her goal statement is to be able to do Saturday morning shopping by herself.

Adam knows how much harder it is to get things done with the kids around. When they first moved into their house, Lisa taking the kids shopping with her made sense. Adam was putting in new hardwood floors in the living room, tearing down old wallpaper, and installing new appliances. It was safer for the children to go with mom. But those projects have been finished for a year. The time is overdue to change the routine to one that is more equitable. Lisa's goal statement, "I want to do my Saturday morning shopping by myself," got the ball rolling. In many ways, Lisa and Adam's goals turn out to be the same: they each want Saturday mornings to be easier, happier, and more fun.

Lisa had been anything but happy for months. Adam knew she was uptight, but avoided bringing it up until she revolted over a TV set going into the garage. To recover some happiness, they had to take small steps. They agreed he would keep both kids at home on Saturday mornings and engage them in activities where he could keep an eye on them. Lisa saved almost two hours by shopping alone and she was a lot happier when she came home. Adam felt that having his wife cheerful again on Saturday mornings was worth the new arrangement. In exchange for Adam being fair, Lisa told him to keep his TV and to finish setting up his man cave.

## Cooperation

Many parents feel stuck in a rut and somewhat hopeless about getting their families back on track. Some want to get right to work on their really big problems. They often have trouble finding the patience to think about strengths and values and don't take the time to make positive goal statements. We know from our research, however, that focusing on strengths helps parents remember why they wanted children in the first place and why they love them so much. And focusing on goals can help solve all kinds of problems in all types of families.

 Daniella and Cesar were skeptical about making goal statements. They were at their wits end and wanted the pain to stop. When asked about their goals for their family, they stated they wanted their children to stop fighting and to do as they were told without arguing. They couldn't imagine how thinking about their strengths and values and identifying goals could improve the behavior of any of their three children—two boys in elementary school, Benito and Miguel, and a daughter in middle school, Ava. They seemed to be at war over something every day. Daniella summed up her feelings like this: "When I tell them to do something, I want them to do it now, and I want them to do it without pushing back. I feel as if the kids are forever fighting with each other or with me. I don't see how making lists about what is good about myself or the kids will get them to stop fighting or pick up after themselves."

Daniella and Cesar had been struggling with the chaos of school-day mornings for several months, with the kids fighting over use of the bathroom they shared. When Daniella was asked to identify a goal to help solve the problem, she started with: "I want our daughter to stop creating such a selfish scene in the morning!"

The problem here is that Daniella's goal describes what she doesn't want. Simply saying she wants Ava to stop her selfish morning dramas doesn't address what she should be doing instead. To design a plan with a chance of success, she needs to start by defining what she wants Ava to do.

Daniella was asked to remember a time when things went well between the children and identify something positive about each child. Cesar helped by remembering that Ava is especially sweet when she reads to her brothers before bed, and both boys like to snuggle up next to her while listening with rapt attention. It was surprising how drawing up that image of the children acting cooperatively changed the tone of the discussion. Even though Daniella and Cesar figured the goal of peaceful mornings would be impossible, they came up with something more realistic: "The children share the bathroom equally and get out the door to school pleasantly." By framing their goal statement positively, they could begin to think of small steps toward the goal.

Daniella began to perk up. "Ava needs to get up on time for starters and share the bathroom."

"And the boys have to stop banging on the door and shouting at her," Cesar added. "Hmmm. Or maybe, stated positively, the boys have to knock quietly on the door and politely ask Ava to open up."

Now that they had clear goal statements, the next challenge was to make bathroom time run more smoothly—no simple task. Maybe they should start with something easier than their number one problem and come back to this after they've had some practice. Our studies show that parents are more successful when they start with something the children already do well, at least sometimes, and then work to make it better.

Daniella and Cesar decided to have the kids practice working as a team doing something that didn't involve limited resources (like one bathroom, limited time, and three kids). They remembered that they do a pretty good job with the dinner dishes. Ava takes the lead at the sink, rinsing the dishes and putting them in the dishwasher. Benito clears the table and wipes off the counters. Miguel puts the pots and pans away. This routine has worked well since the parents made TV and screen time contingent on finishing the dishes.

. . .

What would the steps be in your household? As a parent, envision what you want to happen and turn that vision into action. First, sharpen your focus on your long-term goal. Can you see it clearly? What are some specific qualities or characteristics you can see? Remember, a goal is something a stranger can understand without further details. For example, if you tell your twelve-year-old daughter to "be more helpful around the house," she may be within her rights to respond: "What does that mean? I already do a lot." Try stating the goal like this: "I'd like you to help me with the dishes after supper." This is a clear statement of what you want. Your daughter may still have questions, but your idea of the help you want around the house is quite specific. And you can sharpen that statement even more by saying you want her to clear the table, wipe down the counters, and sweep the floor.

The key is to find your own answers using strategies that work for you. Tailor the strategies we introduce here to fit your family's strengths, values, and dreams.

# Recap

Imagining the family of your dreams means clarifying what you want in the long term and in day-to-day behaviors. You will be most successful if you build on strengths already present in your family—your own and those of your children. When we think about change, we often focus on problems, but stating a problem does not tell us what to do. Use clear and specific goal statements to turn problems into action plans.

## Practice Assignment

- Identify three personal strengths you have as a parent and one or two things that interfere with your parenting.

- Identify one or two strengths for each one of your children.

- Write down one long-term and two short-term goals that you hope to achieve.

# Chapter Two

# Follow My Directions

---

N ow that you have identified family strengths and set some simple goals for family change, let's make a plan to achieve them. Guess what? It starts with compliance. When your children follow directions, they can accomplish a wide variety of goals that become increasingly complex in the months and years to come—doing well in school, showing compassion toward others, and even making the world a better place. Following directions and cooperation are inextricably linked. Parents teach their children to follow directions by providing a strong lead or example.

Cooperation is a cornerstone for learning the skills required to get along in today's world. It emerges as we teach our children prosocial behaviors like following directions, self-care, helping others, and sharing. Ideally, we begin teaching these social skills as soon as children begin developing language and are able to understand our words. Parents need a great deal of patience to shape a cooperative spirit in their children. And that starts with teaching them to follow simple directions like: Come to the table for lunch now, please. Children who learn to follow directions at home are more likely to cooperate with adults and children wherever they go. Most three-year-olds are well on their way to following directions and becoming cooperative.

Isabelle has a robust vocabulary and an insatiable curiosity. She is also strong-willed. Soon after she turned three, she started asking "why" whenever her parents, Kayla and Rick, told her to do something. At first, she wasn't being contrary; she just wanted an explanation. Her questioning elicited repressed chuckles from her parents, a response not lost on the child. Soon she was asking "why" in response to everything her parents asked her to do. Her favorite response became: "No. Why?"

At the same time, Isabelle was teaching her parents to give in with threats of a tantrum. When they said "no," she responded with complaints that quickly escalated into full-scale fits. Recently, she started screaming in the checkout line after her father said "no" to her demand for a candy bar. Surprised and embarrassed, Rick quickly caved in to stop the pain. Isabelle's precocious behavior did not seem as cute anymore. Her parents realized that they needed to start teaching Isabelle to accept "no" and follow directions. The Terrible Twos (and Threes!) were upon them.

Kayla reached her limit one day while making lunch for Isabelle. She called out from the kitchen: "Izzy! It's time for lunch!"

Isabelle heard her mom from the living room where she was sitting on the couch with an iPad in her lap playing her favorite game. She pretended not to hear as she bounced a figure from one red flower to the next.

Kayla finished slicing an apple and arranged the pieces into a smiley face on Isabelle's plate: "Izzy, come on! It's time for lunch!"

Isabelle kept playing. Kayla slammed the plate on the kitchen table and marched into the living room feeling exasperated. Every day, it was same nonsense. Kayla stood over Isabelle and hissed: "Isabelle, I said, it's time for lunch. Get into the kitchen right now!"

"No. Why?"

"Because I said so!"

"Because is not a reason," Isabelle said matter-of-factly.

Kayla finally lost it and grabbed the iPad. Isabelle began crying. Fuming, Kayla pronounced: "No more iPad!"

Isabelle cried harder.

———

What every parent wants (some desperately) is compliance. Kayla simply wanted her daughter to come to lunch. The response she got was noncompliance. Parents' most common complaints have to do with their children's noncompliance. They describe the problem in different ways: their children don't listen; they do as they please; they act stubborn; they don't obey; or they simply say "no." Parents tell us that their children employ a wide array of strategies to avoid compliance. Some argue; some refuse outright; some do what you ask, but with an attitude; some tell you they will do it, but later; and some ignore you. It can really get under your skin, and then you lose control. A certain amount of noncompliance, however, is normal. Remember the study of children from different cultures cited in the Introduction: well-socialized preschoolers comply about 70 percent of the time. As they mature to school age, the compliance rate improves to about 80 percent.

When children disobey and we react in anger or frustration, we set the stage for a battle of wills and that demon coercion rears its ugly head. Young children can be quick to escalate that battle with a temper tantrum. Older children may draw you into an argument or even a shouting match. However the scene plays out, the problem starts when the parent makes a reasonable request that is met with "No." Just as cooperation is the foundation for positive social behaviors, noncompliance is the cornerstone for more serious behavior problems when it becomes a common pattern that carries over to school, friends' homes, and community settings.

## Clear Directions

Parents have different ways to get their children to comply. Many involve coercion, which essentially involves the use of psychological and even physical force to accomplish a goal. "You will do what I say or else!" Stress in our personal lives and in the workplace often ignites our use of coercion. Moreover, for better or worse, we tend to follow examples set by our own parents. If coercion reigned supreme in your family as you were growing up, you may find yourself using it with your own children and also your spouse or partner.

At one end of the spectrum, we've seen parents who command their children like boot-camp sergeants. They may resort to threats or, in extreme cases, even violence. At the other end, we have watched parents, determined not to follow in their authoritarian parents' footsteps, plead with their children over something as simple as coming to dinner or shutting the door quietly. Neither approach is effective, as you may have discovered already. Commanding, debating, or pleading with children does not teach cooperation. What we have learned from watching parents and their children is that the most efficient approach is to give the child a clear, concise direction in a polite, emotionally neutral, tone. It sounds deceptively simple, doesn't it? It is not.

We have developed a set of strategies for giving clear and effective directions that encourage cooperation. Here are our basic strategies.

## Basic Strategies for Giving Clear Directions

- Use good timing.
- Get physically close.
- Make contact (eye contact and/or physical contact).
- Use a pleasant tone of voice and facial expression.
- Give one direction at a time.
- Make a statement—don't ask.
- Be specific.
- Say what to do.
- Use the child's name.
- Use the words "please" and "now."
- Say: "Name, do (behavior) now, please." (e.g., "Isabelle, come to the table, now please"). Use few words.
- Start with behaviors that take less than two minutes.
- Stand and hold silently (with a neutral to positive expression).

This last point, stand and hold, requires that you remain close to your child after you deliver your direction and wait silently for their response. Parents say this is hard to do, especially maintaining a neutral facial expression while silently waiting. Try it and you will see how powerful your quiet presence can be. If you deliver your direction and walk away, you send the message that you may not expect immediate compliance.

Integrating these elements into the directions you give your children can produce amazing results—at least at first. The reward for the parent is compliance. It will come as no surprise that children who learn to follow their parents' directions at an early age also tend to be socially successful with peers, teachers, and others in the community.

We are all guilty of reacting irritably, especially when stressed. Hostility, frustration, and anger are hallmarks of coercion. When you are upset and give these feelings free rein, promoting cooperation is virtually impossible. In stressful circumstances, calm down and ask yourself a few questions: What is my goal here? What do I really want? Do I just want to show my children how angry I am? Or do I want them to follow my direction? If your goal is simply to express irritability, let it rip. And then prepare for the aftermath.

Here's an example that illustrates this point.

You come home from work tired, walk in the door, and there in the middle of the doorway lies an expensive jacket. Your immediate reaction is to lash out, and the one who happens to be there is the person who left the jacket. Do you give your beloved child a pleasant greeting? Or do you shout out: "What is that jacket doing in the middle of the floor? Do you know how much that cost? How many times do I have to tell you—hang your jacket in the closet!" Does your child—does any child—respond by quickly jumping up and hanging up the jacket, then giving you a smile and a big hug? Have you set the tone for a pleasant evening with your family? Probably not. Instead, the combination of jacket and shouts generates a flow of negative reverberations like the ripples created when tossing a stone into a calm pool of water. When it comes to telling your child to carry out this simple task, you tend to be irritated because the jacket should not have been in the middle of the floor in the first place.

---

Let's rewind and consider another way to deal with the jacket.

On the way home from a stressful day at work, you are thinking about how nice it will be to have a pleasant evening with your family. You come into the house, your arms full, and you see your child's jacket lying in a heap on the floor. Your child is slouched on the couch playing a video game. Of course you are irritated! However, you really would like to have a pleasant evening with your family. Your immediate reaction is to lash out. Try using the enhanced steps for giving clear directions below to design an alternative response that will set the stage for cooperation.

---

## Enhanced Strategies for Giving Clear Directions

- *Prepare yourself.* Stop what you're doing and pay full attention to your direction.

- *Get your child's attention.* Say your child's name, get close, use eye contact, use touch (as appropriate).

- *Say what you want the child to do.* Saying what *not* to do omits the necessary information. "Put your jacket in the closet, now please." vs. "Don't leave your jacket in the hall."

- *Make it short and simple.* Use the fewest words possible and make them easy to understand.

- *Make a statement; don't ask a question.* Questions imply choice (e.g., "Pick up your jacket, now please." vs. "How would you like to pick up your jacket?")

- *Pay attention to timing.* Give directions at reasonable times (e.g., not five minutes before your child's favorite TV program is finished).

- *Be calm.* When necessary, take time to become calm in face, voice, language, and body posture. Keep negative emotions under control.

- *Be pleasant, polite, and respectful, but firm.* Show that you expect cooperation in a firm yet positive manner (face, voice, language, and body posture). Use the word "please."

- *Don't allow discussion.* Simply repeat the same clear, short, polite direction. Arguing reinforces noncompliance.

- *Give one direction at a time.* More than one reduces cooperation.

- *Give your child time to respond.* Cooperation means getting started within ten seconds.

- *Maintain contact.* Stand and hold for ten seconds. After that, restate the direction using the same words and neutral-to-positive emotions.

- *Follow through.* When your child complies, praise the behavior with words, smiles, and positive gestures.

Clear directions can have a profound effect on you and your entire family. Most parents require lots of practice to make clear directions a standard habit. It can be shockingly hard. If it were easy, we wouldn't need this book or the years of research it took to figure this out! How you lead as a parent affects the way your child will follow. And, before you can change your child's behavior, *you may have to change your own.* That's right. We can't expect our children to become cooperative unless we are skilled at being calm, clear, and polite in the face of chaos.

Think about how many steps are involved. First, when you saw the coat on the floor, you had to stifle the almost automatic (and actually quite natural) irritated reaction. If you allow yourself to react with anger, how do you think your child will react? And how will you then respond to that reaction? And then how likely is it that you will have a pleasant evening with your family? And, by the way, has the jacket been hung up? So, whether you like it or not, the first person you have to change is yourself.

In our decades of working with parents—and being parents—we have met few moms and dads who automatically knew how to deal with irritating situations. Our human reaction to a biting mosquito is to swat it. Most of us have no idea how often we go through the day swatting mosquitos. Learning to *respond* rather than *react* to life's many irritants is a lesson in self-control that requires practice, practice, and more practice. Automatic negative reactions to pain can be replaced with responses that help you achieve your goals. In the situation above, the goals were a pleasant evening and the coat hung up

Practice giving clear directions that involve simple actions and that can be accomplished in a minute or two—put your shoes away; close the door quietly; or put your backpack in your room now, please. Don't start with cleaning up a catastrophically messy room or washing the dishes from Thanksgiving dinner. Another mistake parents commonly make is to give what we call "stop" directions: "Stop teasing your brother." "Don't do that." Instead, provide a direction for an alternative start-up behavior: "Bring in the mail now, please." Parents who develop a habit of giving clear directions report that this simple step dramatically improves their children's behavior.

## Directions Gone Astray

Here are some of our favorite examples of directions gone astray. With each of these examples, notice the missing elements of clear directions and think of ways to strengthen the direction using the formula: "Name, do X now, please." And then *stand and hold*. By the way, if you have any doubt about the importance of the stand-and-hold element, have your partner or a friend give you a simple direction and remain pleasantly, but firmly, in your personal space until you respond. When we were demonstrating the stand-and-hold technique with a friend, he said he became so uneasy that he wanted to comply immediately.

## The Drive-By

This is a common mistake we make as parents when giving directions. Naturally, we resort to this approach when we are in a hurry. Rather than taking a few moments to follow the strategies for giving clear directions, we forget several elements.

Dad rushes through the room, calls over his shoulder on his way to the car: "Alison! Hurry up! We have to go!"

———

What is missing here? Look at the strategies for clear directions and revise this statement to make it more likely to succeed. How long do you think Dad will race his engine before Alison joins him? Will he have to go back inside and try again? Given that he has to start over, how likely is he to be pleasant (or at least neutral)? Let's rewind and try it again with another approach.

Dad rushes through the room on his way out the door. He stops, comes back, and stands by Alison. He gently touches her shoulder, makes eye contact, and smiles.

"Alison, grab your backpack and let's go now, please."

Then he stands and waits for her to get started.

———

In the long run, which approach takes more time? And which one will elicit that spirit of cooperation you're working to develop?

## Long Distance

Long-distance directions grow out of a combination of obstacles and circumstances, like stairs, large houses, and parents who are multitasking. They have a lot in common with the Drive-By approach described above. At first glance, it seems easiest to just shout out a direction from wherever you may be. The problem is that these kinds of directions are easy for children to ignore. We also do this with our partners.

 Mom calls from another room: "Cara . . ."

(No response.)

Mom calls again, louder this time: "Cara. . . Cara! Do you hear me?"

Cara irritably answers: "What?"

Mom calls: "Help your brother and come down for breakfast!"

(No response.)

Mom calls again: "Cara! Cara! Do you hear me? Cara!"

———————

Unless your child is in the habit of cooperating under most circumstances, stop what you're doing and take the time to deliver your message in person. Personal delivery has the added advantage of enabling you to stand and hold, which adds extra strength to your direction.

## Buried in Words

Too many words surrounding your directions are an invitation to distraction. Your direction loses focus; your child loses sight of what you want; and you are likely to end up in an argument about some extraneous detail. Save extra words, criticisms, and rationales for their own occasions.

Mom: "Josh, what are you doing playing games in the morning? You've been late for school three times this month and you're going to be late again. How many times do I have to tell you! You can't play games before school in the morning. You have to get ready and out the door! Do you want to be late for school again?"

---

What is wrong with this direction? And, what, exactly, does Mom want Josh to do, anyway? Let's rewind and try it again.

Mom walks up to Josh and stands between him and the TV screen. She touches him gently on the knee, looks him in the eye, and smiles at him: "Josh, time for school! Grab your backpack and be on your way now, please."

She continues standing there calmly.

---

## The Guilt Trip

Guilt trips are a tool that we all resort to from time to time. We try to combine a good direction with a morality lesson. Unfortunately, most kids seem to have the natural instincts of litigators: they ignore the direction, which is the point at hand, and find endlessly creative ways to argue the moral issue. Guilt trips seldom elicit quick compliance from anyone, especially children.

Mom: "Ryan, I just tripped over your backpack and nearly fell down! Somebody's going to break their neck falling over the stuff you leave in the middle of the floor. You never think of anyone but yourself. Don't you realize that other people live in this house? Do you even care? What if I hurt myself? Then who would take care of everything? Who would feed you? Do your laundry? Run the errands? You have to pitch in around here. The least you can do is to put your stuff away. I'm not your servant."

. . .

Maybe Mom feels she has done her job by giving her mini-lecture. Maybe she even thinks her son is absorbing the lesson, thinking his mom is right and he should do better. What do you think? Will Ryan jump up and pleasantly put his backpack away? Let's rewind that scene and use the clear directions technique.

Mom trips on Ryan's backpack. She calms herself with some deep breaths and asks herself what her immediate goal is—what does she want Ryan to do right now? She reminds herself to start out by saying something nice, then walks over to Ryan and smiles: "Hey, Ryan! You're home right on time today! Good work!"

Ryan: "I'm trying."

Mom: "I noticed that, and I appreciate it." She takes another deep breath and remembers her simple formula: Name, do X now, please. "Ryan, put your backpack in your room now, please." Then she calmly stands and silently holds.

Ryan: "I'll do it in a minute, Mom."

Mom silently waits ten seconds, then says: "Ryan, put your backpack in your room now, please." She continues standing, with same positive expression.

Ryan: "But Mooooommmmmmmmmmmmmmm . . . Why are you standing there?"

Mom silently continues standing with a pleasant, but firm, expression.

Ryan sighs and gets up: "Oh, okay." He takes the backpack to his room.

Mom: "Thanks honey. You're a good guy."

• • •

The stand-and-hold element in giving clear directions can be difficult, but as we mentioned above, it has an astonishing effect. Notice that Ryan asked why his mom was continuing to stand there. Think of that as a rhetorical question—no answer is required. For most parents, this step takes the most practice. Many children grow uncomfortable when their parents stand in their space quietly waiting for them to comply. When they ask why you're standing there, the best response is no response. Simply continue to stand, silently counting out the ten seconds of your hold. When you reach ten, repeat the direction calmly and pleasantly. Whatever you do, don't be drawn into a discussion, argument, or explanation. Hold your silent ground. Whether or not you maintain eye contact depends on you and your child and the situation. Sometimes eye contact is the right thing to do. At other times it may be the worst thing to do. If stand and hold is challenging for you, practice with your partner or a friend.

## Sarcasm

When you're irritated, it's extremely difficult to give a clear direction. And when you add sarcasm to the mix, you can safely expect an in-kind return—like a fast game of Ping-Pong.

Dad stands over the shoes in the middle of the floor, his arms folded across his chest, a scowl on his face. In an ironic tone, he says: "There they are. As usual."

Ali: "What?"

Dad: "What do you think?"

Ali: "How should I know?"

Dad: "It's your shoes! Your dirty shoes!"

Ali: "Oh, yeah. That's them alright."

Dad: "Get them out of there."

Ali: "And where shall I put them?"

Dad: "You put them away right now or you can just imagine where I'll put them!"

• • •

Take a look at the elements of giving clear directions and help this dad out.

## Questions

Phrasing directions as questions weakens their power and suggests children can choose whether or not to comply. Directions given as statements do not imply choice; they make it clear that you expect your child to do something very specific, and to do it now. Some parents explain that they are trying to soften the effect of a firm, clear directive. But you can be pleasant and respectful without framing your direction as a question. Furthermore, questions sometimes invite irritating responses. Notice how ineffective it is when Dad asks Ali questions rather than making clear statements in these exchanges.

Dad: "How'd you like to pick up your shoes?"

Ali: "Not especially."

*Or*

Dad: "Where do your shoes belong?"

Ali: "In the closet."

Dad: "Well . . ."

> *Or*

Dad: "How many times do I have to tell you to pick up your shoes?"

Ali: "Oh, maybe five or six."

> *Or*

Dad: "Can you pick up your shoes?"

Ali: "No, I can't. I'm busy right now."

––––––

Directions are clear and simple statements, not questions.

## Body Language

Your nonverbal behavior enables you to soften the fact that you are requiring your child to do something now. Tone of voice, facial expression, and body posture all come together to communicate your intention that the child follow your direction, now. See what happens when Dad speaks calmly and stands and holds.

Dad: "Ali, put your shoes in the closet now, please."

Ali: "Aw, Dad. I'm busy."

Dad, in the same pleasant tone, standing and holding: "Ali, put your shoes in the closet now, please."

---

# A Time for Everything

We've been talking about ways to encourage compliance with your directions: get close, make contact, and be pleasant. Now let's talk about *when* you give directions. Even though we know it's not best to give directions in the midst of a TV action sequence or while children are playing a game, we do it anyway. Of course, sometimes we have to interrupt. But it helps to promote a cooperative spirit when you take a strategic approach and wait for a time that has a better chance of catching your child's attention. Take a look at the following list and check the times you think are good for giving your child a direction. Would your child agree with you?

- ☐ During an argument
- ☑ When you and your child are in good mood
- ☐ When your child is in a hurry
- ☐ When you are in a hurry
- ☐ When your child's friends are present
- ☐ When your mother-in-law is visiting
- ☐ In the midst of a tantrum
- ☑ When things are calm

☑ When you are motivated to follow the technique for clear directions

The goal is to engage your children in a positive way, one that increases the likelihood of their cooperation. Stop whatever you are doing and give them your full attention. Tried and true ways to get attention include combining several of the strategies for giving clear directions—opening with a positive comment, getting physically close, making physical and/or eye contact, and speaking your child's name. Starting out with a positive comment enhances the context for cooperation. Sometimes, it's enough to start with a simple: "Hey! What's happening?" It is usually worth the extra effort to listen to their answer. Saying your child's name adds to engagement. Most children respond well to touch that is gentle and nonthreatening. You can touch a shoulder, an arm, a back, or a knee. For children who don't like to be touched, simply enter their physical space, speak their name, and make eye contact. With young children, it helps to bend down and look directly at their faces at eye level.

Considering what we've just learned, let's take another look at the lunchtime scene with Kayla and Isabelle. If Kayla applies the clear directions technique, the outcome will be considerably more pleasant.

Kayla is preparing lunch and wants Isabelle to come to the kitchen. The first thing Kayla does is to walk into the living room. She squats down next to Isabelle, touches her gently on the shoulder, and with a smile says: "Izzy, it's time for lunch. Come to the kitchen now, please."

Isabelle: "No. Why?"

Kayla doesn't react and instead patiently waits with a calm expression on her face. Isabelle looks at her, squirms and whines: "But why?"

Again, without a word, Kayla stands up, maintaining eye contact. In a gentle but firm voice she repeats: "Izzy, come to the kitchen for lunch now, please." Kayla stands calmly, counting to ten under her breath.

Isabelle looks up at her mom. She likes the feeling of her hand on her shoulder and is surprised that her mom isn't angry. She wants to argue some more but, taken off guard by her mom's behavior, she forgets what she was arguing about. She furrows her little brow and tries to think. Mommy said please come to the kitchen. Mommy told her before that people say please when they are being nice. She smiles and puts down the iPad. She takes her mom's hand and walks to the kitchen.

. . .

Kayla ensured Isabelle's cooperation by including all the strategies for giving clear directions. First, she made pleasant physical contact with Isabelle to get her attention. Then her brief, clear words told Izzy exactly what to do: Come to the kitchen now, please. Isabelle (or anyone!) would find it hard to ignore a direction given in this manner. The word "please" modeled the kind of polite behavior Kayla wants Isabelle to emulate. Kayla waited patiently and silently, giving Isabelle the opportunity to respond. The hard part, which requires a fair amount of practice, was to resist answering Isabelle's "why" question. This favorite stalling tactic seldom ends with cooperation. Instead, Kayla controlled her emotions, pleasantly and silently held her ground, and then repeated the direction.

# Recap

Making goal statements a habit will help you create the kind of environment you want for your family. At the most basic level, we want our kids to be happy and to feel secure. Goals help us define the behaviors we want to nurture in our children and ourselves. They give us outcomes toward which we can work. Clear directions let your children know what you want them to do, removing the ambiguity and guesswork of your communications. Now you can start working on teaching your children new behaviors and establishing routines that give your family life structure and predictability—conditions that allow your children to feel secure and thrive.

Parents who prompt compliance with clear directions can avoid coercive interactions and promote a cooperative spirit. They seldom have to resort to commands. Giving clear directions is not a final solution, but it sets you and your family on a good path. This is an important first step in a long chain of change. In the next chapter, you'll see how goal statements and clear directions can help you teach children new skills and habits through encouragement.

# Practice Assignment

Practice using clear directions and take note of your children's response. Choose a fifteen- to thirty-minute time each day to keep track of the quality of your directions and your children's compliance and noncompliance in response. Notice whether or not the quality of your directions affects your children's responses. Count a response as compliance if the child starts following your direction within ten seconds. If not, count the response as noncompliance.

## Tracking Sheet for Giving Clear Directions

Put check marks in the appropriate columns below.

|  | Mon | Tues | Wed | Thurs | Fri | Sat | Sun |
|---|---|---|---|---|---|---|---|
| Good Directions |  |  |  |  |  |  |  |
| Not-So-Good Directions |  |  |  |  |  |  |  |
| Compliance |  |  |  |  |  |  |  |
| Noncompliance |  |  |  |  |  |  |  |

**Examples:**

What went well?_____

_____

What didn't?_____

_____

When did you stand and hold? _____

_____

# What Do Parents Say?

Here are some common responses from parents who have tried our strategies for setting goals and giving clear directions.

- *I was surprised to find such a strong connection between my directions and my child's behavior.* The assignment to keep track of how you give directions and how your children comply teaches you more than words in a book.

- *The instructions for giving clear directions works as well with my three-year-old as it does with my teenager!* Giving clear directions works well for any age group. Teenagers can become rather touchy, so you may want to avoid physical contact, but proximity and pleasant eye contact are good alternatives. On the other hand, physical touch may be necessary to get a young child's attention. The silent stand and hold is often startling to teens and tweens who have learned the pleasure of a good argument. And by the way, this technique works with adults, too.

- *Instead of shouting out a command, I'm actually staying calm, walking up to him, and telling him to do something calmly.* Parents feel better about themselves when they regulate their emotions and tell their children what they want—especially when that extra effort has such a good effect on their children's cooperation.

- *I don't have the time . . .* How much time is spent arguing when your directions are not followed?

- *I shouldn't have to be so careful. They should just do what I tell them, no matter how I tell them.* If your children follow your directions regularly, you don't need this technique. You and your children have already mastered this phase of the art of cooperation. If, however, compliance is a regular problem, strengthen your strategies by giving clear directions.

● *I get so upset when . . . and therefore I can't, won't, don't . . .* Yes, as human beings, we get upset, and then we are not at our best. You may have to change your own behavior to set your children up for success. This is the first law of family cooperation.

● *I thought you were supposed to give children rationales.* Rationales are important. But discussing the reasons why children should put their toys away, help each other, or come to the dinner table are most effective when they take place on separate occasions. Do you really need to explain why it's important to shut the door or turn down the TV? Such verbiage is likely to end up as distraction at best or an argument at worst. If you don't believe this, try alternating using the clear direction technique with a direction that includes a lengthy rationale. Which works better?

● *I shouldn't have to say "please."* Teaching children to use the words "please" and "thank you" begins with parents modeling the way to behave. Sometimes, parents prefer to communicate the essence of "please" through the manner in which they deliver the direction. For example, they may give the direction along with an endearment, such as "sweetie" or "honey."

● *Why should I say "now"?* Some parents feel that saying "now" is dictatorial or authoritarian. Your nonverbal communication can make all the difference in the world. Since you are going to stand and hold until your children begin to comply, you probably want them to get started right away. A reasonable time to wait for a "now" direction is ten seconds. If you think about it, ten seconds is a long time to stand and hold. Try it. At the same time, ten seconds gives your child a chance to recognize that you mean business, and you haven't left the scene of the action. You can give your children a signal that a direction will be coming: "Five minutes until dinner time!" But when you want your children to come to the dinner table, use all the elements of the clear direction technique.

● *I don't like to track things with charts.* Try it out for just a couple of days and determine whether it's worth your while.

● *What do I do when I give a perfectly clear direction and it has no effect?* Don't be alarmed. This is true for many families. In the coming chapters, we'll introduce ways to strengthen the power of your directions.

● *Why do you say "directions" instead of "requests" or "commands"?* We started using the word "direction" because of parents' reactions to the words "command" and "request." Many parents feel that "command" is too authoritarian. "Request," on the other hand, suggests that the child has a choice when choice is not intended. When shoes are in the middle of the floor and you want them picked up right away, you are not asking for a favor or providing choice. You are polite. You are clear. You are reasonable. You give a clear direction, and you expect your child to follow your direction—now, please.

● *If I tell him to put something in his room, but I don't say where, who am I to get mad? He did what I told him to do.* Yes, telling children exactly what you want them to do sets them up to be successful.

● *I used to demand things from my children, not use good manners myself.* Some parents feel that respect should be a one-way street—children show respect to parents, not the other way around. But how do children learn to show respect unless they experience it from their parents?

● *After a while, I didn't feel as if I needed to continue doing the "now, please" routine. Now I only do it when I feel as if they're not really focusing or paying attention.* When your children become accustomed to the direction/cooperation routine, you can relax use of the word "now." If compliance is a problem in your home, however, stick to the technique.

*Chapter Three*

# Accentuate the Positive

---

S o far, you have learned how to set simple goals for your family and how to give clear directions to increase your children's compliance. If you are following these strategies, you should be noticing a positive shift in how you and your children interact. Now we will take advantage of that positive momentum and begin to use encouragement to teach your children new skills. The way to do that is to catch your children being *good*. Even the most obstinate kids do something right occasionally. You just have to look for it.

Our research shows that accentuating the positive side of parenting and minimizing the negative build children's self-confidence and enhance a spirit of cooperation throughout the family. You may not be able to eliminate negativity altogether; problems have a way of creeping into life. But know this—a parent's negative comments carry more weight than praise. It takes about five positive remarks to make up for the cost of a single negative comment. This positive-to-negative balance operates as a kind of bank account. To maintain a positive balance, you have to look for the many small positive steps your children take as they learn the skills for success in today's world. Shining a light on their small accomplishments will nurture the new behaviors that will help them grow. So how do you catch your children being good?

Let's say Kristin, your five-year-old daughter, has been having a bad day and it's starting to get to you. You are in the kitchen unloading the dishwasher while Kristin is having a bowl of cereal at the table. When she finishes, she stands on her tippy toes to put her empty bowl in the sink, but it slips and lands with a loud clunk. The bowl didn't break, but it could have. What does your critical side urge you to do? You could yell: "Watch out, Kristin! Can't you be more careful? You almost broke that bowl!"

· · ·

Okay, let's back up and take a closer look at what just happened. Your daughter was helping you without being told. She was probably feeling good about it, too. Instead of offering Kristin praise for helping, you criticized her for not doing it perfectly. Without realizing it, you just taught Kristin to associate helping out with being scolded. This kind of situation happens among adults as well. If you are criticized when trying to help your boss or a coworker, you probably think: "That's the last time I help that jerk." So what happens if we rewind and turn that situation around to accentuate the positive?

When Kristin puts her bowl in the sink, you have the chance to catch her being good. Seize the moment! Stop what you're doing! Smile at her, and say: "Thank you for putting your bowl away, Kristin. You are such a big help." Your daughter beams a smile in return.

· · ·

It may not seem like much, but by praising her action, you strengthen the odds that she will want to put her bowl away again or do other things to please you. And if you don't want your dishes broken, you can put a small step stool next to the sink.

## Grin and Bear It

Have you ever tried to keep a smile plastered on your face when you are stressed out, tired, and angry inside? Then you know how hard it can be sometimes to accentuate the positive. If you are stressed out and with your children, you have to be extra careful not to let your irritability wipe out the positive balance you've accrued in your relationship account. You know how that goes. Your son does something wrong; you notice his mistake and correct him: "No. Don't do it that way! I told you to fold the towels into thirds like this. How hard can that be?" The positive approach goes something like this: "You're good at folding towels in half. Let me show you a new way that makes it super easy to stack them in the linen closet."

Teaching through encouragement builds cooperation. Encouragement—"Good job! That's how to do it!"—promotes mastery and self-confidence in your children. Children's positive feelings are infectious and will spread throughout the family. We have shown this to be true in our studies for children of all ages. On the other hand, criticism, even when it's constructive, hurts. Most human beings react to pain by striking back, withdrawing, or resisting. Think of your own experiences with criticism. The comments you recall as you're drifting off to sleep are often the negative ones that point out your mistakes or flaws.

Negative comments include criticism, disagreements, and correction. Of course, we have to correct our children from time to time; and yes, we know that disagreements lead to new perspectives. But when it comes to teaching children, it's best to avoid criticism and save disagreements for other times.

It seems to be a universal principle that we learn best when someone sets us up to succeed and recognizes our progress along the way.

When you use encouragement to teach your children, they approach new experiences with a sense of excitement. Whether you realize it or not, you have been using encouragement to teach your children already. Remember when they were tiny tots learning to walk? You held their hands for their first steps. You stood right at their side as they started walking on their own. And they knew just how proud you were because you showered them with smiles and praise. It was easy then. You also found it easy to teach your children language. When they were babies, you played sound games with them, helping them build sounds into words and words into sentences. Using language is one of the most important human activities, and parents are the primary teachers for helping children form this foundational skill. You have shaped the way your children speak and the things they talk about through daily conversation. Did you even notice how often you accentuated the positive?

Depending on their age, you may have taught your children toileting, getting dressed, brushing their teeth, and table manners. Next, you introduced more complicated skills, like playing games, washing dishes, and doing homework. For most parents, teaching complex skills is more difficult because they involve many steps, present different challenges for each child, and require attention and patience to achieve. Children's success depends on their parents' teaching skills and their ability to stay involved.

We have developed and tested two main approaches to teaching through encouragement that work well—tokens and incentive charts. Both depend on your active support for taking small steps on the path to reaching a goal. Tokens are effective for frequently occurring simple behaviors like following directions. Incentive charts help children learn daily routines like going to bed and complex skills like completing a chore. Both approaches involve setting children up for success, encouraging small steps along the way, and noticing and rewarding good behavior. In this way, parents shine the light on what they want to grow. We call this "learning while earning." Here is the basic technique for teaching through encouragement.

## Strategies for Teaching Through Encouragement

- Identify a goal behavior or skill to develop.
- Break the goal into achievable steps.
- Clearly describe each step.
- Tailor steps to the child's abilities.
- Notice and encourage the child's efforts.
- Identify stumbling blocks, then break that step into smaller steps.
- As the child achieves mastery, increase the challenge.
- Reinforce efforts.
- Celebrate accomplishments.

# Tokens

When using a token system, you give children small symbols of your approval for specific behaviors. When they earn a given number of tokens, they can trade them in for incentives that serve as motivators. For some children, social rewards like smiles, hugs, compliments, high fives, fist bumps, and simple words of praise are enough. Other children need an extra boost, especially when they have developed bad habits, the behavior is difficult, or times are stressful. When social rewards don't do the trick, we recommend pairing praise and smiles with tokens. Combining social rewards with tokens increases the value of words and gestures. After a behavior is learned, you can start limiting your use of tokens and rely on social rewards.

A token system can be as flexible as you like, as long as the rules are clear. The first step is to decide what kind of tokens you will use. Here are some suggestions to guide your choices.

## Strategies for Choosing Tokens

- Choose tokens that are fun, so kids enjoy earning them.

- Choose tokens that are immediate, so they can be used right away.

- Choose tokens that are tangible, so kids can touch or see them.

- Choose tokens that are portable, so they can be used anywhere and are easy to have on hand.

- Choose tokens that give a clear message of appreciation.

- Choose tokens that are flexible, so you can adapt them to your needs, as well as your kids' needs.

You already know the kinds of things your children find attractive. Preschoolers and early school-age kids tend to like stickers. They come in the most wonderful varieties, from simple stars and smiley faces to playful critters or space aliens. For older kids, you can use tally marks on a chart or piece of paper. Whatever you choose, tokens need to be portable so you can use them when you are out and about with your children. Scooby Loops, the stretchy loops used to make potholders, can be used as tokens and repurposed into bracelets or wristbands. You can buy them in craft stores by the scores in all sorts of colors. Some parents load their wrists with a dozen or so of these and, when their children earn a token, they transfer one to the child's wrist. Most kids like to choose the color themselves, and the exchange takes place amid smiles and giggles. There are many other kinds of tokens you can use. Some parents carry beans or colored pasta shapes in their pockets. As the child earns a token, the parent can shift it from one pocket to the other, or give it to the child.

At home, you can use tally marks, pennies in a jar, or poker chips. Some children like drawing or pasting stars on a sheet of paper taped to the refrigerator door. Some especially creative parents use clip art to design tokens, creating sports cards, pictures, and other colorful symbols to mark success. The options are limited only by your imagination. Families with several children like to use group incentives, which we will explain later.

## Using Tokens

As you start using tokens, you must first identify specific goal behaviors you want to increase. These should be behaviors that take place frequently and in face-to-face interactions. Favorites include: following directions, using an inside voice (especially when out in public), taking turns, keeping hands and feet to yourself, chewing with the mouth closed, and using polite language. Tokens help parents shape good behavior in the car or in public places like grocery stores, restaurants, and friends' homes. When choosing behaviors, pay attention to your children's ages, temperament, skills, and the particular setting or place. Most parents find it easy to list the behaviors they want their kids to stop (shouting, hitting, slamming doors, talking back, running in the house). Start by listing these problem behaviors as you did in the first chapter. Then, beside them, write the behavior you want to increase, which often is the positive opposite. Use words that fit your family. Identify opposite pairs that make sense to you and your children. Here are some examples.

| ☹ Problem Behaviors | ☺ Goal Behaviors |
| --- | --- |
| Noncompliance | Compliance (following directions) |
| Disobedience | Obedience (following directions) |
| Arguing | Accepting "no" for an answer |
| Running inside | Walking inside |
| Hitting/kicking | Keeping hands and feet to yourself |
| Shouting | Using inside voice |

At home, you can use tokens to encourage behaviors for specific activities. For example, if you're trying to teach sportsmanship when playing games, use tokens for following the rules, taking turns, and making positive statements to each other—"Good job!" or "You're getting the hang of it." At the dinner table, parents use tokens to teach children to chew with their mouths closed, to use the proper utensils, to sit appropriately, and to wipe their mouths with a napkin. In the car, behaviors can include buckling the seat belt, sharing space with siblings, and using an inside voice. In a grocery store, good choices include accepting "no" for an answer, staying close, using an inside voice, and walking rather than running. As you design your token system, think about settings and situations that are the most problematic in your family and choose specific goal behaviors that can solve the problem.

Tokens earn rewards that can come in all sizes and shapes. Moreover, they can be of any value. What serves as a motivator for one child may have no value whatsoever for another. You know best what your children like. As with everything else, your values, as well as each child's age, interests, and preferences, come into play. Later in this chapter, we provide you with a list of incentives that families have generated over the years. However, even this list is limited. Children are usually the best source of information about the rewards they value most. Our grandson loves those dried seaweed snacks. He is more motivated to earn a little box of seaweed than a candy bar. His parents would never have guessed his proclivity for seaweed without asking him what he wanted to earn.

The main point is that the reward must be one that you are willing and able to provide when it is earned, and it must be valuable enough to your child to make it worth earning. It is also important to know that any incentive loses its value when you use it over and over, so you have to change rewards from time to time. Creating a list of ideas in advance helps you keep your child's rewards motivating.

## Designing a Token System

A comment we often hear from parents is how easy it is to tailor token systems to their families. The trick is to design plans that work in different situations. If you are using tokens for a fifteen-minute car trip, children may need only three to five tokens to earn a reward and the reward may be small—a sticker or a treat from the store. If the trip is two hours long, you may require ten or fifteen tokens, and the reward may be larger—fifteen to thirty minutes more screen time or a later bedtime. For even longer trips with several children, divide the goal into parts (every hour, or every two hours) with stops for exercise breaks or treats along the way. If you are using tokens to increase cooperation at home, set your goal and a specific amount of time that will enable you and your child to succeed and offer a reward based on the difficulty of accomplishing the goal. Flexibility is the name of the game.

When starting any new practice with your children, begin by describing how the system works. Your explanation, as always, will depend on your child's age, maturity, and level of functioning. Plan what you will say and chose a pleasant time for the discussion. As you explain, use examples of the positive behavior that you want to encourage and demonstrate its negative opposite behavior. Demonstrating the wrong behavior with humor can make it fun and easier for your child to remember. Always *end* with the positive example you want to encourage, so your children will remember what you want them to do. Show the tokens and talk about the incentives that can be earned. This is the perfect time to build buy-in by asking them what they want to earn and even what skills they want to learn. If they are willing, practice how it works. If not, make sure that the first few times you use the tokens involve easy situations that are quickly resolved.

Here is a strategy for explaining a token system.

## Explaining a Token System

&#9745; Choose a good time to talk.

☑ Be encouraging.

☑ Show your child the tokens.

☑ Describe the behaviors that earn tokens.

☑ Demonstrate good and bad examples, ending with the good behavior you want to encourage.

☑ List several possible incentives and engage your child in making choices.

☑ Explain how tokens earn rewards.

☑ Practice how the system works.

☑ Try out the system.

Remember Isabelle, the three-year-old who responded to her parents' directions with "No. Why?" Kayla, Isabelle's mom, has learned to give clear directions and is pleased with Izzy's improved cooperation. Catching her being good several times a day and rewarding her with tokens has helped her learn to use an inside voice and to ask politely for toys and snacks at home. However, Kayla has avoided taking her strong-willed daughter on trips to the grocery store. There's nothing quite like carrying a toddler kicking and screaming over one shoulder, while hefting a grocery bag over the other. Now that Isabelle is learning to follow directions at home and to appreciate tokens as incentives, Kayla is ready to take her for a test run to the grocery store.

 Kayla is pushing the cart down an aisle of the grocery store when Isabelle sees a bag of her favorite cookies. She looks up at Kayla expectantly, who shakes her head no. Testing the waters, Isabelle snatches a bag of cookies off the shelf and places it in the grocery cart, saying sweetly: "Please, Mommy?"

Kayla puts the bag back on the shelf and firmly says: "No!" The gauntlet has been thrown, and Isabelle is not about to give up.

"I want cookies! I want cookies! I want cookies!" Isabelle grabs the cookies and throws them back in the basket. Her screams can be heard throughout the store.

• • •

Have you ever dealt with a public scene like this? Put yourself in Kayla's shoes. Will you give in to escape the embarrassing tantrum? Frankly, there is no easy exit from this situation. It may be best to wait it out, or take your child home (if you can do it without making things worse). Kayla can't let Izzy have the cookies. If she gives in, she will teach her that tantrums produce sweets. In fact, Izzy's tantrum is a prime example of coercion in action. By submitting to the unpleasant behavior to turn it off, Kayla actually reinforces it, teaching Izzy that all she has to do is to up the level of pain to get what she wants.

Kayla chose to leave the store without any groceries. Driving home with her pouting daughter, Kayla realized she had forgotten an essential step: She did not explain the token system and set Isabelle up for success.

The next day, when things were going well at home, Kayla sat down with Isabelle and described the system as a fun game to play in the store.

 Kayla starts on a positive note: "Today when we go to the store, we are going to play a new game. You can earn a treat when we leave the store if you follow three simple rules. Each time you follow the rules, you get one of these tokens."

"Like at home when I listen and put away my toys?" Isabelle asks.

Showing Izzy the colorful wristbands she had put on her wrist before starting the conversation, Kayla says: "Exactly. You're listening so well right now, you just earned one." She slips a pink band on Isabelle's wrist.

"My favorite color!" Isabelle enthused.

"And if you get ten loops while we're in the store," Kayla continues, "you'll get a treat when we finish shopping."

Isabelle asks: "What's the treat?"

"I was thinking about a box of animal crackers," Kayla suggests, "or maybe a Popsicle. How does that sound?"

Isabelle immediately counters with: "How about a blueberry muffin?"

"Well, a whole muffin might be too much before dinner," Kayla responds. "Maybe we could divide it in half, and you could have the second half after dinner."

Isabelle agrees: "Okay. How do we play this game at the store?"

"The rules are really simple for a big girl like you," Kayla says, keeping it positive. "First, you need to stay with me all the time so I can see you."

"But I like to explore," Izzy says.

"You can explore as long as I can see you," Kayla replies. "And I'll give you a loop for staying with me. Okay?"

Isabelle agrees reluctantly: "I guess so."

"The second rule is to use your inside voice," Kayla goes on. Then she raises her voice as an example, shouting "Is this an inside voice?"

Isabelle giggles and says: "No."

In a normal voice, Kayla asks: "Is this an inside voice?"

Isabelle, still giggling, responds: "Yes."

Kayla goes on: "And the last part of this game is that when I tell you 'No,' you accept it."

Isabelle folds her arms over her chest and frowns: "You mean if I ask for something and you say 'No,' I can't have it?"

Kayla smiles and answers: "Yes, that's right. Here's what you do instead. You say, 'Okay Mommy.' And then you think about something else. And because it's so hard for you to accept 'no,' I'll give you *two* loops."

Isabelle hesitates, then asks: "What should I think about?"

Kayla, sensing the beginning of cooperation, suggests: "Think about the treat you're going to earn as we leave the store."

Isabelle agrees: "Okay. I can do that."

• • •

Kayla first tried out her new system with a short trip to the store to pick up two or three items. Before going into the store, she reviewed the game with Isabelle, armed herself with tokens, and discussed the treat to be earned. While in the store, Kayla paid close attention to Isabelle's good behavior and was generous in giving her tokens. Once, when Isabelle seemed on the verge of wandering away, Kayla called her back, reminded her about staying in sight, and gave her a token for following the rule.

## Group Incentives

The example of Kayla and Isabelle is straightforward because it involves a single child. In families with two, three, or more children, you may need a group incentive. This requires children to work together to earn a reward.

Kate, a mother of three children ages five, seven, and eight, used tokens whenever she had to take the children with her to the grocery store. She started out by explaining at home that tokens could be earned for cooperating while at the store. Kate's rules were simple: accepting "no" for treats in the store earned one loop; helping Mommy retrieve an item on her shopping list earned another loop; talking nicely to each other earned another loop; behaving while in line at the register earned yet another loop. If the children earned fifteen tokens as a group by the end of grocery shopping, they could stop for ice cream on the way home. Kate said her system allowed for flexibility in that she expected the two older children to earn more tokens than the youngest. An added benefit was that her oldest child stepped in at the store to remind his sibs, nicely, to behave. By pooling their efforts, all of the children were motivated to cooperate with each other toward the common goal of ice cream. Activity-based rewards like stopping at the park on the way home, continuing work on a puzzle, or fifteen minutes extra screen time work as group incentives as well.

Here are some additional tips for using tokens to shape your children's behavior. Remember, a token system is a fun way to give immediate recognition for small behaviors like following rules, following directions, taking turns, or closing doors quietly.

## Sample Token Behaviors

☑ Keeping hands and feet to yourself

☑ Following directions

☑ Taking turns (in a game, in conversation)

☑ Accepting "no" for an answer

☑ Using polite language

☑ Holding on to the grocery cart

- ☑ Coming to dinner when called

- ☑ Appropriate behavior in the car

- ☑ Buckling up

- ☑ Using an inside voice

- ☑ Sharing a travel game with a sibling

- ☑ Positive greetings ("Nice to see you.")

- ☑ Appropriate conversation topics

- ☑ Using positive talk

- ☑ Asking for permission

- ☑ Getting up on time

- ☑ Volunteering to help out

- ☑ Staying within your personal space

- ☑ Showing interest; asking follow-up questions

- ☑ Accepting redirection

## Incentive Charts

Incentive charts and token systems share many of the same elements, but the way you apply them is different. Tokens encourage simple behaviors; incentive charts are for more complex skills. Both spell out an agreement between parent and child, describing how the child can earn specific rewards for specific behaviors. Incentive charts, however, are for routines with multiple steps, like cleaning the bedroom, bedtime or morning routines, feeding an animal, or doing homework. Parents let their children know exactly how to follow a given routine, and children earn praise and rewards as they complete the task. Incentive charts require more work than token systems when you first set them up. Once you have established one or two, the routine becomes second nature. Here are our strategies for designing an incentive chart.

## Strategies for Creating Incentive Charts

- Identify a goal behavior.
- Break the behavior into small, achievable steps.
- Clearly describe each step.
- Tailor the steps to your child's abilities.
- Notice and encourage your child's efforts.
- Identify stumbling blocks, then break the behavior down into smaller steps.
- Make a menu of incentives for your child to choose from.
- Explain the program.
- Reward effort and accomplishments along the way.
- As your children achieve mastery, increase the challenge.

Now let's look at how to integrate these elements into a workable incentive plan.

## Breaking Down Complex Goals

Goals that are more complex require attention to detail. While a simple behavior can be taught with a token system, a complex behavior requires learning a series of steps and combining them properly. Helping children learn a complex behavior calls for breaking the steps into simple patterns, learning them one at a time, and fitting them together. Think of some goals for your children, keeping in mind their current stage of development. For young children, the goal may be to use the toilet or to brush their teeth. For older children, the goal may include chores like cleaning their bedroom, feeding the dog, or washing the dishes.

It helps to start with goals related to skills or routines you want your child to accomplish independently. Make sure that your first goals are relatively easy to learn in a week, or two or three weeks maximum. Make a list of routines, chores, skills, or habits you want your children to carry out on their own. Fit the goal to each child's age, personality, skills, and level of functioning. Just as you did with tokens, engage them in the process of identifying potential incentives.

The challenge is to start with a goal that is not too easy, but not too hard. Remember the Goldilocks rule? Begin with small challenges that build a sense of mastery. Soon, children learn to enjoy taking on more difficult challenges. Below is a list of parents' favorites. Add your own ideas.

## Examples of Goals and Challenges

Morning routine
Bedtime routine
Wash dishes
Fold laundry
Practice musical instrument
Tidy living room
Make bed
Clean bedroom
Set table
Take out garbage
Feed animal
Vacuum floor

Take two or three goal behaviors that are a "just-right" challenge and break them into five easy steps. As you break down the goal behavior, think about your child's current level of skill and make sure each step is easy enough to accomplish. Here are some examples of routines broken into five easy steps.

## Clean Bedroom

1. Make bed.

2. Put toys in toy box.

3. Put dirty clothes in laundry basket.

4. Put clean clothes in closet/drawers.

5. Sweep/vacuum floor.

These steps may be too difficult for younger children. If so, start with simply making the bed. Some parents include a start or stop time as one of the steps.

## Make Bed

1. Pull up sheet and blanket.

2. Smooth sheet and blanket.

3. Put pillow at top of bed.

4. Put stuffed animals on top of bed.

5. Be done by (specify time).

Great teachers notice when youngsters encounter stumbling blocks and turn each stumbling block into a new goal behavior that they break down in turn. Parents help by anticipating stumbling blocks or recognizing when a child has encountered one. Let's take the goal of establishing a bedtime routine. Kevin is six years old and in kindergarten. Getting up on time in the morning is quite a problem on school days, so Kevin's parents decided that he should be in bed with lights out by 8:00. Keep in mind that you want your children to be as independent as possible in this process. Here's how Kevin's parents started out as they broke the bedtime routine into five steps.

## Bedtime Routine

1. Start at 7:30.
2. Put PJs on.
3. Complete bathroom routine.
4. Say prayers.
5. Lights out at 8:00.

Steps 1 and 2 were easy for Kevin, but the bathroom routine turned out to be a giant stumbling block. Kevin enjoyed playing in the sink, making soap bubbles everywhere but on his hands and face. And when he was done, he left the bathroom a mess. His parents decided to break that step—that stumbling block—into several smaller steps and teach him the bathroom routine separately. These are the steps they created for him.

## Bathroom Routine

1. Wash face and hands with soap.
2. Brush teeth for two minutes.
3. Floss.
4. Wipe off counter.
5. Put towel/washcloth on rack.

It took a couple of weeks for Kevin to master the bathroom routine. Then his parents made the bathroom routine a single step on the way to bed.

# Success Grows with Small Steps: Bedtime Routine

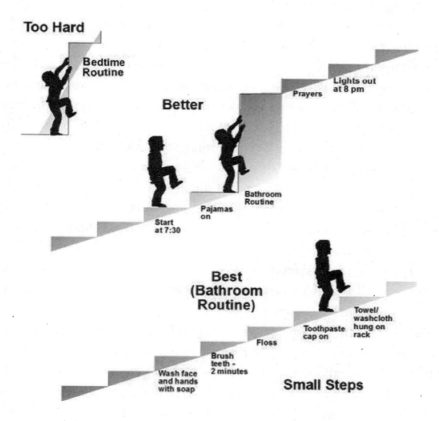

**Too Hard**

Bedtime Routine

**Better**

Prayers

Lights out at 8 pm

Bathroom Routine

Pajamas on

Start at 7:30

**Best (Bathroom Routine)**

Towel/ washcloth hung on rack

Toothpaste cap on

Floss

Brush teeth - 2 minutes

Wash face and hands with soap

**Small Steps**

# Setting Up Rewards

The opportunity to earn a reward each day motivates children. Perfection is not the goal. Remember the 70-percent rule. We suggest you use this as the criterion for earning a daily incentive. This allows children to forget a step or two, but still experience success. Setting kids up for success is always the goal when teaching a skill or routine, and it is particularly important when you start a new program. Evaluate your child's progress after one week and make adjustments. As children master a given skill, consider changing up the system. You can adjust the chart and make it a little harder by combining steps and adding a new step or two. Once your child is consistently successful at completing most or all of the steps, move on to new challenges. You can replace this skill, routine, or chore with something new. Some parents like to include the newly learned skill as a single step on a more advanced chart, as was the case with the Kevin's bathroom routine.

Daily incentives should also follow the Goldilocks rule: the rewards must be small enough for parents to be willing and able to provide them on a daily basis and big enough to motivate children to work for them. Make a list of three or four rewards that your children can earn each day with a 70-percent benchmark for success. Be sure to have several options for a reward, because the same incentive every day becomes boring. Rewards may include treats, privileges that don't cost money, privileges or things that cost money, and parental time. Keep in mind that some daily rewards are not options during the school year, except on weekends. As you generate your reward menu, include incentives from several categories, which will provide you with much-needed flexibility. For example, when you can't spend parental time that your child has earned, you can offer an alternative, like a free pass from a chore or staying up an extra thirty minutes at bedtime. You may not want your child to earn extra screen time more than once or twice a week, but it can be an occasional option.

Flexibility is the key. Most families find it helpful to ask their children to include items on the list. As a parent, you get to set limits on these choices. A new bike is *not* an option as a reward for cleaning the bedroom. Resist the temptation to replace daily incentives with a weekly reward.

Below is a list of potential incentives that includes suggestions from scores of parents. Decide which ideas may work for your children. Social reinforcers help you *maintain* good habits your children have already developed. When you use them, your children understand that you notice and appreciate their efforts. Tangible rewards are stronger than social rewards. They motivate the extra effort required for children to learn *new* behaviors and good habits. You can rearrange the list according to the age of your children and the type of reward you want to give—food treats, parental time, or special privileges. Some rewards are appropriate as a weekly or weekend reward; others can be used most days. Ask your children to help you add to this list.

## Social Reinforcers

☑ Pat on the back

☑ High fives, knuckle bumps, fist pumps, thumbs up

☑ Words of praise: "Awesome!" "Amazing!" "I really liked _____." "Way to go!" "Thank you for using _____." "I love that you just said/did that."

☑ Words of reinforcement: "You must have thought about that a lot." "I'm so proud of you." "Good idea." "Mature decision!"

☑ Secret handshake

☑ Hugs—you did something well

☑ Good touch

☑ Smile

☑ Be happy

☑ Positive physical touch

- ☑ Smiling
- ☑ Positive nickname (Rock Star, Bud)
- ☑ Use their language to praise

## *Tangible Incentives*

- ☑ Food treats your child likes (candy, soft drinks, etc.)
- ☑ Extra bike time (specify the amount)
- ☑ Extra electronics time (ten- to fifteen-minute increments)
- ☑ Trading cards
- ☑ Lip gloss, nail polish; getting a new hairdo
- ☑ Special time with you doing what your child wants to do
- ☑ Picking a game for game night; playing card games with you
- ☑ Having a friend over for dinner
- ☑ Being chauffeured or riding "shotgun"
- ☑ Going on errands
- ☑ Getting to choose _____
- ☑ Baking or cooking with others
- ☑ Free pass for a chore
- ☑ Time with friends (specify)
- ☑ Later bedtime or curfew (specify)
- ☑ Taking a friend on a family activity
- ☑ Going to the Y, gym, or library

- ☑ Treat from store or money for a treat at school

- ☑ Time to pursue a hobby or activity like scrapbooking

- ☑ Buying an app

- ☑ Picking dinner or food rewards

- ☑ Renting a game

- ☑ Watching a movie with you

- ☑ Gas money or gift card

- ☑ iPod cards or iTunes purchase

- ☑ Extra phone time

When assigning points for earning incentives, simplicity enhances success. Experience has taught us that five steps and ten points is a simple target and does the job. Most first graders can count to ten, so one approach is to assign two points to each of the five steps. A slightly more complex approach is to assign one point to the easiest step, three points to the hardest, and two points for each of the remaining three steps. We don't recommend assigning four points to a single step, because, if the child fails the four-point step, he or she cannot earn an incentive that day, even if every other step is completed. Design your system to fit your family's values. After several successful charts, some parents give partial points for a given step. Others require that a step be done properly; then they provide the designated number of points. Giving partial points provides for more flexibility.

## Designing Incentive Charts

An incentive chart is basically a contract that spells out an agreement between parent and child for earning rewards by learning goal behaviors. It lists the routine or task along with the steps necessary to succeed. You can place a box beside each step for showing the maximum number of points that can be earned. The example given below provides a place to record the number of points needed to earn a reward, the possible incentives that can be earned each day, and the time to review the chart. You can also add a menu that can include "daily specials" for variety.

Specifying a time to review an incentive chart helps both parents and children remember to review the chart each day and provide the incentive to be earned. Without daily review, the whole program will fail. It is easy to review the chart on a day-by-day basis when you set it up like this.

Here are some simple steps to follow for setting up an incentive chart, followed by a sample chart you can use as a model.

## Setting Up an Incentive Chart

1. Determine the daily goal behavior or routine.

2. Break the behavior into five small steps.

3. Write the steps on the incentive chart.

4. Assign points for each step.

5. Create an incentive menu.

6. Determine the number of points needed to earn an incentive.

7. Explain the chart.

8. Teach and practice the behaviors.

9. Start using the chart.

10. Review the chart daily and assign rewards as earned.

Page 75 provides an example of an empty incentive chart you can use as a model for your own.

## Sample Incentive Chart

| Name: | | | | Week: | | | | |
|---|---|---|---|---|---|---|---|---|
| Routine/task: | Points | Mon | Tues | Wed | Thurs | Fri | Sat | Sun |
| Step 1: | | | | | | | | |
| Step 2: | | | | | | | | |
| Step 3: | | | | | | | | |
| Step 4: | | | | | | | | |
| Step 5: | | | | | | | | |
| Daily Total: | | | | | | | | |

| Total points needed: | | Review time: | |
|---|---|---|---|
| Possible Incentives: | _____ • _____ • _____ | | |

Now let's look at an incentive chart for a specific goal behavior.

James is an eleven-year-old boy whose parents are divorced. Before the divorce, his mom and dad, Stacey and Steven, had established a routine that worked well. But, as some of us have learned, undergoing a divorce can be stressful on everyone in the family. After the divorce, James began having trouble with his homework. Rather than starting with the homework issue, however, his parents established a new after-school routine and helped it along with an incentive chart.

James had been accustomed to having his mom home when he returned from school, but now Stacey has a job that keeps her away on weekday afternoons. Her absence threw James off of his normal schedule, and he began playing video games after school rather than doing his homework. So, Stacey and Steven agreed to meet for coffee to iron out the details of how they would approach the problem.

Stacey suggested that James be put to work doing chores until she could get home from work. Steven thought chores would feel too much like punishment and wanted to lighten up the new afternoon duties. They compromised on a plan in which James would be free to play his video games after he completed a simple routine.

• • •

Page 77 shows the incentive chart Stacey and Steven developed for James.

## James' Incentive Chart

| Name: James | | | Week: October 11–18 | | | | | | |
|---|---|---|---|---|---|---|---|---|---|
| **Routine/task:** **After-school Routine** | **Points** **10** | **Mon** | **Tues** | **Wed** | **Thurs** | **Fri** | **Sat** | **Sun** |
| **Step 1:** Change clothes | 2 | | | | | | | |
| **Step 2:** Dirty clothes in laundry; clean clothes put away | 2 | | | | | | | |
| **Step 3:** Afternoon snack | 1 | | | | | | | |
| **Step 4:** Clean desk | 2 | | | | | | | |
| **Step 5:** Organize homework materials | 3 | | | | | | | |
| **Daily Total:** | 10 | | | | | | | |

| Total points needed: | 7 | **Review time:** Before dinner |
|---|---|---|
| Possible Incentives: | | 30 min extra screen time • 30 min later bedtime • 99¢ app |

Stacey and Steven developed this chart to provide a new routine for James' after-school time. In addition to providing structure to his afternoons, the activities, particularly cleaning his desk and getting his homework ready, prepared James to do homework when his mom came home. As Stacey and Steven had agreed, the activities posted on the chart combined chores with a snack and followed the Goldilocks rule—not too much work and a daily reward to motivate him. Before implementing the incentive chart, Stacey sat down with James and explained the program. To get his buy-in, she asked him what kind of incentives he wanted. He suggested extra screen time after homework and the purchase of a cheap app. He also liked his parents' idea about a later bedtime. For James, it was just the right combination.

Because every family is different, incentive charts offer a customizable structure. Each parent can design programs that fit each child's unique skills and needs. At first, it may seem that setting up an incentive chart is a lot of work. But it becomes easier with each new chart, and the charts can promote that spirit of cooperation you are seeking.

As with all teaching interactions with your children, the success of your incentive chart depends on your ability to explain the system you are using to your children. It is always worth the time to talk through your expectations and encourage your children to participate in the process. Here are some guidelines for explaining the incentive chart system to your children.

## Explaining Incentive Charts

1. Choose a good time to talk.

2. Be encouraging.

3. Show the chart.

4. Explain each step on the chart.

5. List the points for each step.

6. List several possible incentives and engage your child in making choices.

7. Explain how points earn incentives.

8. Explain the number of points needed to earn a daily reward.

9. Set a time for daily review.

10. Start using the chart.

11. Adjust the chart as necessary, but try it for a week before making changes.

# Recap

In this chapter, you have learned strategies for encouraging behavior: tokens for frequently occurring simple behaviors and incentive charts for more complex skills. Teaching your children to follow directions and develop new skills is no easy task. Tokens and incentive charts can help you teach them what you expect and provide them with encouragement as they develop good habits. It's a labor-intensive process as you start, but it simplifies life and enhances cooperation in the long run. In the next chapter, you'll learn how to keep your cool and maintain emotional control while honing these critically important skills.

## *Practice Assignment*

Review the steps for creating and using token systems and incentive charts. Then use the worksheets below to develop either a token program or an incentive chart. Parents with younger children usually start with token systems. Resist the temptation to mix the two together, however. And remember to follow the guidelines given above for explaining token systems and incentive charts to your children.

## Creating a Worksheet for Token Systems

### Step 1: Identify a setting.

List 3 or 4 settings in which you want to improve behavior: the grocery store, in a car, on a bus, playing with friends, at the mall, visiting relatives, anywhere.

_____    _____

_____    _____

### Step 2: Identify positive behaviors to encourage.

List some behaviors you want to encourage. Start with behaviors that are important, doable, not too difficult, and that happen often. Identify a short time (e.g., 30–60 minutes) when you will encourage these behaviors. Sample behaviors: following directions, hands and feet to self, taking turns, buckling up in car, sharing with sibs/friends.

_____    _____

_____    _____

### *Consider:*

- ☑ How often might these behaviors occur in a setting or during an hour
- ☑ When is the best time
- ☑ How you will stay positive
- ☑ What may interfere
- ☑ How you can plan for contingencies

Select the top three positive behaviors to start with.

## Step 3: Select a token.

Choose a token that will suit the setting, your child's age and preferences, and ease of use. Sample tokens: stickers, tally marks, body stamps, Scooby Loops, plastic chips, points.

### *Consider:*

☑ Are they easy and fun to use?

☑ Are they easy to keep track of and total up?

☑ Are they easy to keep with you?

☑ Are they the same for all your children?

## Step 4: Make a menu of possible incentives.

Write possible small incentives. Take a look at the page of sample incentives; ask your child.

_____   _____

_____   _____

_____   _____

_____   _____

Circle the ones you want to keep; cross off ones that won't work.

## Step 5: Determine how many tokens earn an incentive/reward.

☑ Make it easy to win.

☑ Catch good behavior early and often.

☑ Perfection is not required.

## Step 6: Explain the token system.

- ☑ Focus on your child's strengths.
- ☑ Show the tokens.
- ☑ Go over the rules.
- ☑ Go over the incentives and get more ideas from your child.
- ☑ Give reward at the end of the hour.

## Step 7: Teach and practice the behaviors.

- ☑ Model the behaviors; show your child how to do them.
- ☑ Role Play: Have your child practice the appropriate behavior several times.

## Step 8: Identify what you can do to promote success.

- ☑ What will make it easy for your child to be successful?
- ☑ What are some challenges or barriers to success?
- ☑ Can you remove barriers?

## Step 9: Start the token system.

- ☑ Set your child up to be successful. Prompt if necessary.
- ☑ Be consistent and encouraging.

## Step 10: Provide earned rewards.

- ☑ At the end of the specified time, review tokens earned.

- ☑ Provide incentive.

- ☑ Don't take away an incentive that was earned, even if your child's behavior gets worse.

- ☑ Shine the light on what you want to grow! Focus on the positive.

- ☑ If your child did not earn enough tokens for a reward, comment on positive things he or she did. Say: "I bet you'll do better next time."

## Step 11: Troubleshoot and make adjustments as needed.

- ☑ Am I giving my children directions that are clear, calm, and short?

- ☑ Am I encouraging?

- ☑ Do I give incentives when they are earned?

- ☑ Are the incentives motivating?

- ☑ Am I doing what I need to do to help my child be successful?

## Creating a Worksheet for Incentive Charts

### Step 1: Determine a goal behavior to teach.

List chores or routines you want your child to learn to do well.

_____          _____

_____          _____

Circle one for your first incentive chart. Select a chore or routine that your child can do easily. Success is the goal!

### *Decide the following:*

☑ When will the task/routine happen (start/stop time).

☑ How often will it happen (daily, weekdays)?

### Step 2: Break the behavior into five small steps.

1. _____

2. _____

3. _____

4. _____

5. _____

### *Consider:*

☑ Can your child do what is asked?

☑ Are the steps specific?

☑ Are the steps small enough?

**Step 3: Write the steps on the chart.**

**Step 4: Assign points to steps (five steps).**

1. Assign number of points per step (i.e., a total of 10 points).

2. Perfection is not required. The goal is 7 out of 10 points earned (70-percent rule).

3. Assigning points places value and emphasis on each step.

4. Understanding point values prepares children for the world of monetary values.

5. Children become familiar with learning-earning approach.

**Step 5: Create a menu of possible incentives.**

Brainstorm possible small, daily incentives:

_____     _____

_____     _____

Cross off the ones that won't work and circle the ones to keep.

**Step 6: Identify how you can help your child be successful and encourage him or her.**

☑ What tools, help, things will your child need?

☑ How can you "set the stage" for your child to be successful?

☑ What are things that will make it easy for your child to be successful?

☑ What are some challenges or obstacles to success and can these be removed?

## Step 7: Explain the chart.

- ☑ Set a time.
- ☑ Be encouraging—focus on what the child is doing well.
- ☑ Show the chart.
- ☑ Explain each step.
- ☑ List points.
- ☑ Go over the incentives and get more ideas from your child.
- ☑ Say how points earn incentives.
- ☑ Set a time for daily review.

## Step 8: Teach and practice the behavior.

- ☑ Model, demonstrate what you expect your child to do.
- ☑ Have your child practice the behavior several times.

## Step 9: Start the chart.

- ☑ Set your child up to be successful. For the first two to three days, stay close and go through routine with your child, prompting if necessary.
- ☑ Be consistent in using the chart and expecting that your child will do the behavior.

**Step 10: Review daily.**

☑ Pick a consistent time to review the chart—after school, before dinner, immediately after task is completed.

☑ Identify that time here: _____

☑ Provide incentive as close as possible after review.

☑ If child is not successful, find positive points to accentuate. Say: "I bet you'll do better tomorrow."

**Step 11: Troubleshoot and make adjustments as needed.**

☑ Are my directions clear, calm, and short?

☑ Are the steps small enough?

☑ Are we using the chart every day?

☑ Am I encouraging when we review the chart (even when all points aren't earned?)

☑ Are incentives given when they have been earned?

☑ Are the incentives still motivating?

☑ Am I doing what I need to do to help my child be successful?

# What Do Parents Say?

Some parents embrace the idea of adding tokens and incentives to their routine. Others resist. Still others try it out, have some success, and then let it slip. Here are some common responses from parents who have tried these techniques.

- 🗨 *Now I encourage my children. Before there was no encouragement.*

- 🗨 *The best thing I learned is praising them for doing a chore. It makes them happy, and the next time, they do the chore again.*

- 🗨 *I realized that children need incentives to feel motivated and do things better. Just as we ask for a salary raise, and we do things better with a raise, children need incentives.*

The structure of incentive charts helps both parents and kids. Here's what four parents said:

- 🗨 *I used to say to my son: "Clean up your room!" If he didn't, I punished him. Now, I use the five steps on the incentive chart. I sit down with him and explain to him what I expect and put the chart on the fridge. All this helped me to become a better mother.*

- 🗨 *Breaking behavior down into steps helped me teach my child how we wash dishes, sort clothes, clean the bedroom. I've learned that the simpler you keep it, the easier it is and the more likely they will be able to do it.*

- 🗨 *Even when my son didn't contribute anything at home, I used to give him money and let him go out anytime. Not anymore. Now he needs to complete chores or else I don't give him any money. The incentive chart helped me, because I was a very permissive parent. Now, with the incentive chart, I motivate my son. He feels good and contributes more.*

- 🗨 *I think the biggest success we had was using the stickers, using the Scooby Loops, that kind of stuff. And then not having to use them anymore because it was working.*

Most parents are pleased to discover that, once their children become cooperative, they don't have to rely so much on using incentive systems to teach new behavior. But when problems emerge, remember to accentuate the positive and avoid shifting into negative mode.

Some parents initially resist the idea of rewarding children for specific behaviors. When they try out the token or incentive system, they are often pleased with the results. Here are some of their questions, along with our responses.

- *Why should I reward my children for doing what they ought to be doing in the first place?* You are using incentives to promote goal behaviors that either are not happening or are not happening the way you want them to. Rather than nagging or scolding your children, you are encouraging them, and this contributes to a cooperative atmosphere in the family.

- *Won't too much praise/encouragement weaken my children's character?* Parents who encourage their children as they learn new skills empower them. Children look forward to trying new things and are not afraid to make mistakes.

- *Our kids already have everything they want. What more can we give them?* Children value incentives more when they work to earn them than when they are given to them at no cost.

- *Nobody rewards me for doing what I'm supposed to do. Why should I reward them?* Do you receive a salary at your workplace? Would you continue your job without pay? Your children's workplaces are at home and in school. Earning while they learn builds their sense of mastery and self-confidence.

- *We give our kids all we can afford! What if we can't give them more?* Financially strapped parents often feel guilty because they can't give their kids things they want. Take another look at the list of incentive examples. You'll notice that many things cost nothing.

- *I'd rather have my child earn a weekly reward, not a daily one. Every day is just too much trouble! What do you suggest?* Remember, we're not talking about adults. Children find it hard to wait for earned rewards, especially if they are young and impulsive, or struggle with the task. As children learn to break bad habits, learn new skills, or complete difficult tasks independently, immediate rewards work best.

- *Do weekly rewards work too?* Weekly rewards are a nice way to motivate sustained practice. For example, some children earn a weekly reward for being successful on their incentive chart for five or six days. They also receive their daily reward when it's earned.

- *What do I do when my children don't earn a reward?* Remain encouraging. Normalize occasional failures and focus on the future. Remind them that they will have another opportunity tomorrow and change the subject.

- *Should I withhold the reward if my child has earned it, but then misbehaves?* Never withhold an earned reward. You can provide a negative consequence for the misbehavior, but keep negative sanctions separate from earned incentives.

- *What do I do when I'm too busy to give the promised reward?* Take another look at the incentive examples and see if there isn't something that doesn't require your time. Remember, the key to success is that the reward is something you are willing and able to give and that has value to your child.

- *How long do I have to keep using incentives?* When your children master a goal, move on to a new behavior, or increase the level of difficulty.

# Chapter Four

# Oceans of Emotions

---

B y now, you know how setting goals, giving clear directions, and using incentives can work together to reduce tensions and increase your children's cooperation. Although using these skills may be easy when you're in a good mood, it can be difficult, if not impossible, when you are frustrated, in a sour mood, worried about money, or experiencing anything that affects your emotions negatively. In fact, don't be surprised if you forget everything you know about parenting the next time you trip and fall over the child-size sneakers left in the hallway. Learning to regulate your emotions may be among the most challenging things you do in family life. As with other things, all it takes is practice.

We know that our emotions—or more precisely, our failure to control them—often get us into trouble. Emotions are integral to how we act and react with our children and partners. We can't eliminate them. What we can do, however, is become more aware of our negative states and get a hold of ourselves. This is important, because the way we express our emotions with our children has a powerful and direct effect on their thoughts and feelings.

In this chapter, we'll explore strategies that can help you be mindful of your feelings and your children's feelings, and regulate your emotional expressions. No one can be in a good mood all the time, and there's nothing like a spat with a child to bring out the worst in any of us. Here, you'll learn how to catch yourself being negative and shift your mood into positive, or at least neutral, territory. Cue the song *Put on a Happy Face.*

# Emotions Have Consequences

Positive emotional expressions and gestures, like a smile or a tender pat on the back, serve as powerful reinforcers for messages. They say: "I like that." "I love you." "That was a good idea." "Thanks for picking up your coat." On the other hand, a scowl or a snarl can turn the very same words into something your child interprets as critical or hurtful. The emotions you attach to your words and your body language are more important than many realize, especially when you're telling a story, listening to your children talk, setting limits, or imposing discipline on your child. In fact, five decades of studies show that few parents can use discipline effectively until they have learned to regulate their emotions.

Our emotions have far-reaching effects on our children. Some parents are better at controlling their emotions than others. The test of your own skill lies in how you behave when your children misbehave or refuse to follow your directions. In these moments, it's all too easy to become upset and snap out orders instead of giving clear directions. When you express anger toward your children, they are almost certain to react defensively. You snap; your child snaps. And pretty soon, there is nothing but snapping and sniping until someone gives in. This is a coercive cycle—a little "rubber band" conflict that tends to build up, putting us, as well as our children, at risk of losing control. The goal is to prevent these kinds of coercive situations in the family. Once they happen—and they will—you need strategies to end them quickly.

 Traffic was backed up on Susan's commute from work. As she started to call home to say she would be late, the screen on her cell phone went black. The charger was not in the glove box, which meant her husband, Stan, had lost his again and taken hers. What a jerk, Susan thought as she glared at the endless string of cars crawling in front of her. But at least Stan might make it home before her and start dinner. When she finally pulled into the driveway at 6:30, Susan felt a tinge of relief at the sight of Stan's car. Briefcase in one hand, purse in the other, and laptop case slung over one shoulder, she opened the front door and sniffed for the scent of something—anything—cooking. Nothing. Her spirits fell and her frustration rose, like swells in the ocean before a wave crests and crashes.

"I'm home!" Susan took three steps through the doorway and tripped. "What the…" The strap of her laptop case slid off her shoulder, causing her to drop her purse and spill its contents across the floor. After regaining her balance, she looked down. A pair of boy's sneakers lay tangled at her feet. "Justin! Justin!" Her ten-year-old son came running from the hallway. His cheerful smile evaporated the moment he saw his mom's pinched expression and his sneakers lying in the foyer.

"How many times have I told you not to leave your shoes in the middle of the floor!" she bellowed. Stan popped out from his den, saw the spilled contents of his wife's purse, the sneakers, and her frown. He knew that look. Nervously, he asked: "Hey, what happened?"

"Where's my charger?" Susan snapped back. "And why haven't you started dinner?" She glared again at her son. "I said pick up your shoes! I nearly broke my neck."

Stan and Justin avoided further eye contact with the angry woman in front of them.

· · ·

But what if Susan gives herself a chance to regroup before reacting? What if, instead of immediately giving in to her frustration, she manages to catch her balance and take a couple of deep breaths, enough time to diffuse the bomb about to go off inside her. Work stress, traffic jams, dead cell phones, and low blood sugar are a potentially toxic combination.

Fortunately, however, Susan has been practicing controlling her emotions at home for several months. Most of us are good at regulating emotions in the workplace, because we know the consequences of yelling at our bosses or coworkers are serious. The trick is learning to pause before reacting.

Let's rewind and see how Susan can better address this situation.

 Susan turned around and walked back to the car, leaving the contents of her purse on the floor. She sat down in the driver's seat to regain her composure, took a dew deep breaths, and called on her skills at making goal statements. "What do I really want to happen at home tonight? I want a peaceful evening with my son and husband." She pictured how, two nights ago, the three of them were laughing and talking about their day during dinner. "How can I make that happen tonight?" she considered. "I can walk back inside, avoid the shoes, pick up my things, say hello pleasantly, and sit down." With her goal in mind, Susan re-entered the front door.

Stan and Justin were already kneeling on the floor, picking up the loose change, wallet, makeup, and other items from the purse.

Susan smiled down at her husband and son. "Hi. Thanks for picking up my stuff."

"Are you okay?" Stan asked innocently.

"I'm fine, thanks. Justin, pick up your shoes and put them away now, please," she said.

"Sure, Mom. Sorry about that."

"What held you up? I tried to call and you didn't answer," Stan said.

"Let's talk about that later," Susan replied, taking a seat on the couch. "Oh, what a day! Anything for dinner?"

"We only got home a few minutes before you," Stan said. "What if I order takeout?"

. . .

Susan had good reason to be irritable. Who wouldn't be? However, blasting her family would not make for a pleasant evening. Imagine the chain reaction. One irritable response would beget another, and the hostile interchange could escalate into a conflict that would leave bitter feelings lingering over the family for hours or even days.

Instead of reacting and starting a fight, Susan made the conscious decision to take control of her emotions. She left the scene to interrupt the anger. She calmed herself by imagining the type of evening she wanted. She wanted to enjoy a few relaxing hours with her son and husband. And she wanted a dinner she didn't have to cook. That's all. She delayed a conversation with Stan about her missing phone charger and said nothing about dinner not being ready—which was a good thing, since Stan had been running late, too. By not reacting and taking a few moments to think about what she wanted to happen, she was able to avoid a major fight. Stan and Justin knew they had both dodged a bullet and were extra nice to Susan that evening.

## Regulating Emotions

Notice that one step Susan took to calm herself was to consider her goals for the evening. Goals help you think about what you want in the future, rather than focusing on the problems that are staring you in the face. Typically, you want those problems to stop *now*. Goals help you focus on what you want to happen *instead*. If you want a fight, go ahead and express your irritation. A fight will follow as surely as day follows night. If you want to enjoy family time, take a moment to cool off. Then you can think about your goal without negative words or feelings. In fact, exaggerate your goal by putting it into dream mode. When you can create positive images in your mind, you take control of your emotions, direct your attention to the future, and identify what you want. You may be surprised by how much you can influence what happens next.

Here are some strategies for helping you regulate emotions that are threatening to get out of control.

## Strategies for Regulating Emotions

- Respond; don't react.

- Disengage physically—walk away or go to another room.

- Disengage mentally—count to ten; take deep breaths.

- Lighten the situation—change the subject; use humor.

- Empower yourself—remind yourself you can manage this.

- Focus on the positive goal you want to achieve.

- Join the other person—understand your child's perspective; actively listen.

- Express positive emotions—smile, focus on your own best feelings, those of your child, or something good in the context.

No doubt you are thinking that this is easier said than done. And you are right. When you are upset, you really *do* want to act on it. It takes practice—lots of practice—to calm your inner dragons. Actions and reactions become habits, and habits are hard to break. Be forewarned that, when you're upset, the way you think about things tends to lead to poor decisions. Studies of interactions between parents and their children have found that, as soon as one person (parent or child) introduces a hostile comment into the stream of interaction, productive thinking comes to a screeching halt, making it likely that the family will have a fight and the problem under discussion will be left unresolved.

When you're trying to deal with family problems, conflict leads to unresolved issues, and that leads to increased stress. Increased stress leads to increased irritability, and more unresolved problems. This is often how families become entrapped in coercive interactions, because they cannot or will not control their negative emotional expressions. Negative exchanges erode love. Coercion is like a corrosive acid that destroys the opportunity to promote a cooperative family atmosphere. To keep the family in harmony, you have to remove the source of the acid. To keep the love in your family from eroding, you have to reduce or stop the coercive conflicts.

Learning to control or regulate your emotions is healthy not only for you, but for your whole family. Regulating emotions reduces levels of stress hormones in the blood and helps keep your blood pressure from spiking into the stratosphere. It also reduces fear and confusion in your children. We've heard moms and dads say that fighting is good for their relationship and that they're simply blowing off steam when they yell at each other. Unfortunately, children don't understand that concept. All they hear are loud and angry voices, and they tend to assume that their parents' fighting is their fault. Most couples argue, but it's best to keep it out of earshot of your kids. If you think they aren't listening or can't hear you arguing from the other side of the house, think again.

Bruce and Teresa have been married for nine years and have two children, seven-year-old Sammy and five-year-old Mia. They say they have a good marriage, though both admit they have short fuses and are quick to escalate minor squabbles into shouting matches. Teresa describes it like this: "We have our own *style* of arguing, and I'm sure it sounds like World War III is breaking out to our neighbors. But it's just our way of getting whatever is bothering us out of our systems. Then we drop it and move on."

However, Sammy and Mia do not move on as easily. Every time their parents start yelling, they become filled with anxiety and often end up shouting at each other over trivial issues—just like their parents. Bruce and Teresa had no idea how much their fighting affected their children until they got a call from school. Sammy and another boy had an argument during recess and Sammy's shouts were so loud that everyone on the playground stopped in their tracks. After Sammy stopped yelling, he sobbed for several minutes and had no idea why he was so upset.

The school counselor suggested that Bruce and Teresa look into therapy for Sammy to help him get control of his emotions. As their faces burned with embarrassment, they exchanged knowing looks. On their way out the door, Teresa whispered to her husband: "I think we're the ones who need therapy."

On the drive home from school, Bruce and Teresa tried to keep the mood light and offered to take the kids out for pizza. Over dinner in the noisy, but cheery pizza parlor, the parents brought up the shouting fit at school.

Bruce said: "We have noticed how you and Mia have started to yell at each other the same way you yelled at that boy. Mommy and I think that our arguing has set a bad example for you kids, so we will try to change our behavior."

"Why do you and Mommy fight so much?" Sammy asked.

Teresa answered: "We don't know, Sammy. It's become a bad habit."

"Are you and Daddy getting a divorce?" Mia asked. "I don't want you to divorce." Then she started crying.

Teresa hastened to reassure her: "Oh no, honey. Daddy and I love each other very much, just like we love you and Sammy.

Daddy and I have to teach ourselves to control our emotions and stop raising our voices."

"What do you mean by emotions?" Sammy asked.

Teresa and Bruce looked at each other and took a deep breath. Teresa began: "Well, emotions are the feelings we get when something good or bad or surprising happens. Like when you get in trouble for something at school, how does that make you feel?"

"Mad at myself," Sammy said.

"Okay, what if you get in trouble, but it was someone else's fault?" Teresa prodded.

"I get mad at the teacher," Mia chimed in.

Teresa followed up: "All right. Mia, how do feel when Sammy breaks one of your toys?"

"Mad. And maybe sad, too," she said, "'cause the toy is broken."

"And if Sammy says he is sorry and offers to fix it?" Teresa asked.

"I guess then I'm not mad anymore."

Teresa took her one step further: "What if Sammy gives you a present? How do you feel then?"

"Happy?"

"That's right," Teresa said. "You see, we can have lots of different feelings depending on what happens. What we have to learn to do when we are mad is to cool off before we say or do anything. That is what Daddy and I are going to practice every time we feel like yelling. If we take some time to cool down, then maybe we won't yell so much. Daddy and I didn't realize we were upsetting you so much and teaching you that it's okay to yell at each other. We will set a better example for you," Teresa promised.

Bruce chimed in: "One of the things about growing up is learning to think before you speak. How about the next time someone feels like yelling, we all take a break. Later on, when we're calm, we can sit down and talk about it."

Mia nodded. "Okay," she said. "And maybe you should put a quarter in the swear-word jar, too."

"That's a deal," Teresa agreed.

• • •

Bruce and Teresa added our guidelines for regulating emotions into their smartphones so they could consult them whenever they were tempted to launch into an argument. Moving forward, they taught their children some cooling-off tricks as well. Fortunately, they were wise enough to accept and even embrace their responsibility for setting the emotional tone of the family. Otherwise, their children might have earned reputations as short-tempered and loud.

We can't expect our children to regulate their emotions if we can't or won't regulate ours. It's best to tackle these common obstacles one at a time. When you do, you begin to see how closely many of the behavioral issues your children face are tied together. The first step for Bruce and Teresa was to make a plan to change their own behavior rather than getting angry with their children or the school counselor. All that was required to avoid this pitfall was a little self-regulation.

## Controlling Negative Emotions

Let's look at the many ways negative emotions creep into our family lives, starting with those occasions on which our children do not comply with our clear directions.

Once again, your daughter Maggie left the milk on the counter. It feels as if she will never learn to put it away. Last week, she spoiled a half-gallon of milk! Her carelessness is driving you crazy. You can feel your blood pressure rising. You remember to take a break before you follow your instinct to shout at her. The milk can stay there a few more minutes while you compose yourself.

Music is your favorite way to calm down, so you put on some tunes and listen for a while. Once you feel better, you walk over, sit beside her, and ask her what she had for snack. After listening for a while, you touch her on the shoulder and pleasantly say: "Maggie, put the milk in the refrigerator now, please." Maggie changes the subject and seems not to have heard you. You calmly stand up, look her in the eyes, and firmly but pleasantly say: "Maggie, put the milk in the refrigerator now, please." And you stand quietly, thinking to yourself : I can do this, I can do this. Maggie gets the message and puts the milk in the refrigerator. As she does it, you congratulate yourself on your self-control and pleasantly thank her.

· · ·

The big question is what to do when you give clear directions and they don't work, even when you have played your part perfectly. First you have to regulate your emotions. In the next chapter, you'll learn how to blend discipline into the parenting mix. In the meantime, just avoid getting into an argument that will simply give your child justification for noncompliance.

A situation that often calls for regulating emotions occurs when using tokens or incentive charts. When children fail to earn enough points or tokens for an incentive, they may attempt to coerce you into giving it to them anyway. You can prepare yourself by thinking through the situation. Your child is going to be disappointed and may whine or even throw a tantrum. Consider how you will deal with this. You can acknowledge your child's disappointment and mention that tomorrow will present another opportunity to earn the reward. Then direct the child toward an alternative activity and walk away.

How do you steel yourself for the mini thunderstorms that take place every day? If you engage in them, you reinforce them with your attention. Knowing that you can disengage using your favorite self-soothing device is the secret to success. This reminds me of a YouTube video I saw in which a child is throwing a tantrum. The mother leaves the room. The child stops, looks around for his mother, runs into the room where his mother is, and starts the tantrum all over again. This wise mother walks away again. And guess what happens! That's right. The child suspends the tantrum until he regains his mother's attention. Tantrums attract attention, and they often get specific rewards—a treat that was denied or soothing attention. As long as safety is not an issue, tantrums are usually best left to wear themselves out. The big question for parents is how on earth to maintain sanity during the tantrum or in other situations in which children escalate emotions to get their way.

## Cooling Off

Parents helped us develop the list given below of strategies to regulate emotions in difficult situations. Here, we've separated those strategies into six categories in order to consider each in greater detail. The ones you choose to use will depend on the circumstances and your personal interests, talents, and style. You may already have some of these strategies in your repertoire, but it helps to have a wide variety of options. Some will work best when you can't leave the scene; some will work well with younger children; some will work well when you're with your partner or spouse. Finds the ones in each list best suited to your situation, then add more to the list. We also give you a list of things you should *not* do when caught in an emotion-fraught situation.

## Disengage physically:

- ☑ Leave the scene.
- ☑ Go to your room.
- ☑ Go to the bathroom.
- ☑ Take a walk.
- ☑ Text yourself.
- ☑ Put on headphones.
- ☑ Send your child from the room.

## Disengage mentally:

- ☑ Count under your breath.
- ☑ Take deep breaths.
- ☑ Recall a pleasant scene.
- ☑ Take your pulse.
- ☑ Listen to music.

## Lighten the situation:

- ☑ Change the subject.
- ☑ Use humor.
- ☑ Gather information.
- ☑ Offer choices, all of which are acceptable.
- ☑ Offer a compromise.

## Empower yourself:

- ☑ Tell yourself, "I can manage this."
- ☑ Focus on your goal.
- ☑ Objectively observe the situation.
- ☑ Plan ahead and prevent the problem.
- ☑ Learn from the experience.
- ☑ Respond, don't react.
- ☑ Slow things down.

## Join the other person:

- ☑ Understand their perspective.
- ☑ Stand in their shoes.
- ☑ Actively listen.
- ☑ Acknowledge your role in the problem.
- ☑ Paraphrase.
- ☑ Use positive body language.
- ☑ Summarize.
- ☑ Notice the person's positive qualities.

## Strengthen positive emotions:

- ☑ Focus on the positive emotion of the other person.
- ☑ Mirror the other person's positive emotion, smile.

## Other strategies:

_____

_____

_____

## Don't:

☑ Don't give unwanted advice.

☑ Don't interrupt.

☑ Don't defend yourself or react blindly.

☑ Don't criticize.

☑ Don't jump to conclusions.

As you consider these strategies, I'm sure your thinking once again: Easier said than done. But there are a number of simple things you can do to defuse emotional situations and bring down the emotional temperature of a bad situation. Here are just a few. Try one or two, then ask yourself if there are other ways that will work for you.

## Strategies for Cooling Off

☞ *Physical exercise* is a great way to disengage from conflict and engage in something that is healthy. Moreover, it generates endorphins, which not only help to calm you, but also add to positive feelings. Some parents tell us that they enjoy cooking as a cooling-off strategy.

☞ *Make positive self-statements.* Tell yourself: "I can do this." When you tell yourself you can't do something, you set yourself up for failure. Apply the same tools to yourself that you use with your children. Identify your own stumbling blocks and break goals into smaller steps.

- *Empower yourself* by stating what you want in the future in a positive manner. Most likely, your goal is seldom to start a fight; but a fight is what you get when you lash out at someone you love. If you want to generate a spirit of cooperation and spread it throughout your family, consider what steps you can take to help everyone get there. Write down your goals and keep them as a "to do" list.

- *Go somewhere quiet* for a few moments and recall a pleasant experience. It helps to close your eyes and imagine the scene. Were you inside or outside? What time of day was it? What were you wearing? Try to remember the sounds and smells of that time. You may be surprised to find yourself with a smile on your face in just a few minutes.

- *Prepare ahead of time* for difficult emotional situations. You may not be able to anticipate exactly how things will unfold, but you can plan a strategy or two to use for dealing with different contingencies. Visualize yourself calmly addressing the situation. Put icing on the cake by imagining how good you will feel when you have managed it well.

- *Step back and observe* a stressful situation as if you were a total stranger. This increases your objectivity and helps you understand another's perspective. Some parents say it helps them see the situation from their child's perspective. This is difficult to do when you're upset, so try it when you are in a good mood. Better yet, watch some other family trying to deal with a similar situation.

# Increasing Positive Emotions

Let's turn now to think about increasing positive emotions—showing interest, taking pleasure, and being affectionate or caring. Practice sharing positive emotions with your partner or your children when things are going well. Pay attention to how they convey their feelings and try to mirror their positive expressions. If your daughter is telling you a story about something funny that happened at school, lean toward her and try to match her facial expression. Or if your son is telling you about something that concerns him, maintain eye contact, keep your tone of voice calm and interested, and ask questions that allow him to respond. Remember to pause after each question to give him a chance to talk. Hard as it may be, try not to give advice while you are in the listening phase. If you can make yourself pause long enough, your child may even ask for your advice.

Stressful conditions can lead to feelings of anger, fear, sadness, or some combination of these. When stress is chronic, expressing negative emotions becomes almost second nature, preventing you from addressing the very challenges that cause stress in the first place. People develop different styles of reacting to stress. Angry people can express themselves in a dramatic and straightforward fashion, which can be terrifying, or at least upsetting, for the people around them, especially children. Some people mix anger and anxiety or mask anxiety with aggression. No doubt, you have noticed this pattern in dogs—usually rather small ones that confront potentially frightening situations by charging forward, barking fiercely, and baring their teeth. As soon as the "dangerous person" reacts by stomping a foot and making a threatening gesture, the dog turns tail and races away, sometimes even whimpering. We call this the "fear-biter" approach. You probably know some people like this.

Another reaction to stress, especially when it becomes chronic, is depression. Depressed people tend to assume a negative perspective on the world and focus on shortcomings—their own and those of their children. They are not optimistic dreamers prepared to befriend change. They are inclined to feel overwhelmed and hopeless about the future.

Negative emotional reactions to stress are normal, and even useful sometimes. However, anger, depression, and anxiety tend to evoke negative reactions from others. When you develop a habit of responding to situations with negativity, you may soon find yourself without supportive friends, or your friends may learn to match your negativity. Our research shows that the homily about birds of a feather is all too true. Happy, well-functioning people like to be around others who are cheerful. Angry, irritable people tend to hang out with—you guessed it—others who are similarly unpleasant. And positive people tend to avoid depressive people altogether.

Recognizing signs of how your children may be feeling enables you to respond accordingly. For example, if your son is anxious, you want to make him feel secure. If your daughter is angry, you may want to give her space until she calms down before you talk with her. And if your child is sad, you may need to show some empathy. As parents, we tend to want to make the problem go away, so we slip into problem-solving mode before we take the time to recognize and respond to our children's feelings. This can be unhelpful, and it takes a certain amount of control on our own part to avoid it.

Emotions are not intractable. You can regulate your emotions, just as you do when you adjust the thermostat in your home. There are many techniques that work—some of them fairly simple and some requiring considerable practice. The ability to dial down your negative emotions is a foundational parenting skill for setting limits for your children's behavior. Dialing up positive and even neutral expressions makes it easier to give clear directions, teach through encouragement, be positively involved with your children, and solve problems, large and small, that arise in all families.

Let's be clear, however. Being positive (or at least neutral) when you feel negative is hard work. It takes commitment and self-control. As your children more willingly follow your directions, master new routines, and build self-esteem, you will find your days getting brighter. Being positive will start to become second nature. The first step in regulating your emotions, as you already know, is being mindful or aware of them and preventing yourself from reacting thoughtlessly. Once you do that, you can become a supportive sounding board for your children when they need understanding and advice. Teri's story is a good example.

Teri works as a marketing director for an IT start-up. Her days are long, and she spends much of them listening to her CEO rant about the company's stock price and blaming her for not attracting more investors. One evening, Teri came home with her boss's whiny voice still echoing in her exhausted mind. Her teenage daughter greeted her at the door and said: "Something's up with Troy. He's been in his room since he got out of school, and he didn't touch his snack."

Teri's first thought was: "Oh please. Not today." Troy had just started seventh grade, and he seemed to love it. Whatever was bothering her twelve-year-old son couldn't be *that* bad and certainly not as stressful as what she had been through that day. Her daughter hugged her goodbye as she left to spend the evening studying with a friend. When Teri went upstairs, she noticed that Troy's bedroom door was closed and the TV was on. To add to the frustrations she was putting up with from her boss, Teri was also irritated that her husband was on another work trip—his third in a month. She really wanted to close her own bedroom door, collapse on the bed until morning, and let Troy fend for himself. But she pulled herself together to move on with the evening. She still had work to do, so she decided to order out for dinner. She changed out of her work clothes, then knocked lightly on her son's door. "Hey, are you in there? I'm home."

Troy opened the door and looked glumly at his mom. "What?"

"I hear you didn't eat anything after school. How about I order us a pizza?"

Troy stared expressionless at his mom, his shoulders slumping. "Whatever."

Teri thought to herself: "Fine. I hope you stay in your room the rest of the night." Instead, she could see that her son was upset and put her irritations aside. "What's going on? I can see something is bothering you."

"Nothing. I'm fine," Troy said flatly.

Teri prodded gently: "Okay. Can you tell me a little bit?"

Troy's face blushed red. He stood in front of her without speaking for what seemed like an eternity. Teri had to fight back another wave of irritation. She smiled and lightly touched her son's shoulder.

Troy started to open up: "My teacher called on me in history class, and I gave the wrong answer. Everybody laughed at me."

Teri looked surprised. "Oh? Didn't you do your homework?"

Oops. Wrong response. Troy shot his mom an angry look. "I did my homework, but when the teacher called on me, I got nervous and forgot the answer. Geez!" Troy shrugged his mom's hand off his shoulder. "She doesn't get it," Troy thought. He wished his dad were home. He would understand.

• • •

How many times has your own emotional state led to a misunderstanding with your child? It happens all too often, especially when we're tired, stressed out, and barely have enough energy to manage our own needs. Teri wanted to be sensitive to Troy, and she started out well. She understood that his slumping shoulders and glum looks were signs that something bad had happened. However, she wasn't ready to listen. She was hungry and tired. A better time to talk may have been after dinner when blood sugars had bounced back into human range. Standing in the hallway was not the best approach either. Then, instead of lending him a sympathetic ear, she accused him of wrongdoing, thereby shutting down discussion. Let's rewind to see what happens when she steps back and waits until they both have had some food.

 Teri felt her face flush and, once again, had to calm her emotions. Troy started to back away into his bedroom, ready to slam the door.

"Troy, I'm sorry," she began. "I forgot to leave my job at the office. Let's start over. I'll order us a pizza. What toppings would you like?"

"I don't care," Troy mumbled.

"Okay. How about I order one with everything but anchovies?"

"Sure," Troy answered as he returned to his room and the TV program. Teri turned on some soothing music and did a brief yoga workout while waiting for the pizza. Dinner was rather quiet, but neutral. Finally, when both of them were comfortably full, Teri relaxed into her chair and tried again.

"So you said that when the teacher called on you, you forgot the answer. Did something make you nervous?"

"Yeah," Troy admitted reluctantly.

Teri waited a moment, then said: "I'd like to hear about it if you want to tell me. What made you so nervous?"

After another long pause, Troy let it out: "There's this girl in my class, and I think I like her. I was kind of staring at her when the teacher called on me. I couldn't remember. And then she laughed, too."

"Oh, I bet that was embarrassing," Teri responded. "What's her name?"

"Carina."

"That's a pretty name. How long have you liked her?"

"About a week."

Teri smiled and said: "I bet you wanted to impress her. Did that make you nervous?"

Troy nodded.

Teri gently inquired: "Was she nice to you today?"

"Yeah, but I feel so stupid."

Taking a deep breath, Teri went all in: "You must like her a lot. Tell me about her."

• • •

With that, the floodgates opened and Troy confided to his mother about his first crush and his confusion about girls. If Teri had stayed focused on her own bad feelings, she would have missed the opportunity to hear about her son's first infatuation. Notice that, earlier, her bad mood led her to jump to an accusation rather than to seek more information. When you are in a negative state, you tend to think negatively about what is happening now, in the past, and even in the future.

## Indicators of Emotions

Parents often ask how they can read their children's emotions. Below is a list of common indicators for the primary emotions of sadness, contempt, fear/anxiety, anger, happiness, interest, and affection/caring. You will probably recognize most of them. However, parents say that it's reassuring to check the list sometimes when they aren't certain. It can also help to know the indicators for positive emotions, especially when you are working on increasing your own expression of interest or caring. Familiarize yourself with the indicators. Learn to be sensitive to your children's moods and to recognize when something is troubling them. Become your family's "child whisperer."

Research has identified dimensions of emotional expression that appear consistently across cultures. This outline provides ways of detecting emotions based on this research. The indicators given are just that—*indicators*. They may or may not be present. But you may find it helpful to be familiar with these signs.

## Negative Emotion Indicators

### Sadness/Depression

- ☑ Tone of voice—very quiet, sometimes whiny, resigned, bitter

- ☑ Body language—downcast eyes, slumped posture, defeated appearance, weight of the world on shoulders

- ☑ Sighing

- ☑ Mildly tearful to crying/sobbing

- ☑ Withdrawn

- ☑ Negative mood

- ☑ Tendency to notice negative and not positive aspects of people or situations (glass half empty)

- ☑ Looking down often

- ☑ Pauses in speech when not expected

- ☑ Low energy level—excessive fatigue, lethargy, wiped out, slowed down

- ☑ Trouble concentrating

- ☑ Trouble eating—too much or too little

- ☑ Trouble sleeping—too much or too little

- ☑ Feelings of worthlessness or excessive guilt

- ☑ Feelings of hopelessness or helplessness

## Fear/Anxiety/Stress/Tension

- ☑ Tone of voice—tightness or tension in the voice, sometimes too loud, very fast pace

- ☑ Facial expression—widened eyes, flushed, mouth open and drawn back

- ☑ Body language—jerky, tight, rigid, or stiff

- ☑ Keyed up, agitated

- ☑ Jumpy

- ☑ Feelings of numbness

- ☑ Hypervigilant

- ☑ Excessive startle reactions

- ☑ Inappropriate laughter

- ☑ Restlessness

- ☑ Extremely high activity levels

- ☑ Itchiness

- ☑ Shortness of breath

- ☑ Lump in throat

- ☑ Trouble concentrating
- ☑ Avoidance of people, situations, and objects that provoke fear
- ☑ Picking words carefully, as if conversation is dangerous

## Contempt/Disgust/Scorn

- ☑ Using put-downs, insults
- ☑ Character assassination
- ☑ Curled lip with raised cheeks
- ☑ Asymmetry of facial expression (e.g., one corner of mouth tight)
- ☑ Rolling of eyes
- ☑ Hissing (like gas or radiator steam)

## Open Anger

- ☑ Tone of voice—loud, shouting, hostile, abrupt, biting, hissing, clipped, sputtering
- ☑ Facial expression—tight and narrowed eyes, pressed lips, furrowed brow, V eyebrows, bared teeth
- ☑ Body language—threatening gestures, forward leaning, high energy
- ☑ Increase in volume or rate of speech, often with a key word stressed
- ☑ Blaming, hostile words

## Constrained Anger

- ☑ Tense

- ☑ Unsuccessful attempts to appear rational

- ☑ Definite edge to voice

- ☑ Stiff body and tight face

- ☑ Pressed lips

- ☑ Forced, "unfelt" smile

## *Positive Emotion Indicators*

### Happiness/Enjoyment/Pleasure

- ☑ Can be shown silently or audibly

- ☑ Varies from mild happiness to ecstasy or joy

- ☑ Corners of lips are drawn up and back

- ☑ Mouth may or may not be parted, with teeth exposed or not (smile, broad grin)

- ☑ Sounds of pleasure (e.g., chuckling, giggles, laughter)

- ☑ Wrinkle runs down from nose to outer edge of mouth beyond lip corners

- ☑ Cheeks raised

- ☑ Crow's-feet wrinkles go outward from outer corners of eyes

Note: Smiles are often used to mask other (often negative) emotions.

## Interest

- ☑ Tone of voice—warm, relaxed, calm, inquiring

- ☑ Attentive energy

- ☑ Strong physical cues (e.g., leaning forward)

- ☑ Positive facial expressions (warm, soft, curious)

- ☑ Change in energy from passive to active listening

- ☑ Eye contact given by interested party

- ☑ Inquiring, but not intrusive

- ☑ Questions that allow the other person to respond (e.g., pause after the question)

- ☑ Paraphrasing in a question format

- ☑ Seeking clarification

- ☑ Uses engaging words (e.g., Tell me more! Really? Is that so)

## Affection/Caring

- ☑ Tone of voice—warm, soft, sweet, kind

- ☑ Direct physical expressions of caring

- ☑ Comforting

- ☑ Appears peaceful, mellow, contented, friendly

- ☑ Voice sometimes slows, with a drop in amplitude, though with a definite intensity or energy

- ☑ Loving/caring statements (e.g., "I love you," "I care about you.")

- ☑ Reminiscing, sharing moments that increase closeness

- ☑ Compliments

- ☑ Statements that communicate pride or support

- ☑ Pet names said in warm tone of voice

- ☑ Indications of empathy

- ☑ Mirroring feelings that show understanding or shared feelings

# Recap

Let's take a look at the progress you have made so far. A lot of you have probably become so adept at giving clear directions that you are doing it with your coworkers, friends, and relatives. Next, you began using encouragement with the aid of incentives to teach new behaviors. You likely have noticed how each skill builds on the next. In this chapter, we introduced specific techniques for recognizing and managing your emotions, which will increase your effectiveness using the skills you have learned so far. Best of all, you will be able to keep your cool while everyone around you is losing theirs. You are strengthening your parenting foundation.

## *Practice Assignment*

Before moving on to the topic of discipline, take this opportunity to practice your skill in recognizing and regulating emotions. Try paying close attention to at least two emotional situations—one positive and one negative. This exercise will help you learn to both experience an event and observe it somewhat objectively. Begin by reviewing the indicators of emotions. Then use the Regulating Emotions Rating Form to help you evaluate the details of each emotion you chose to study. Select one positive emotion (happy, joyful, interested, friendly, affectionate, loving, calm) and one negative emotion (angry, irritable, depressed, sad, fearful, anxious, worried, disgusted, contemptuous). As you complete the form, re-envision the event and describe it in detail. Becoming more aware of emotional situations and the strategies you use to regulate them will give you greater control. Remember to focus on your successes, not your shortcomings.

## Regulating Emotions Rating Form

**Positive Emotion (happy/glad; interested/friendly; neutral/calm; affectionate/supportive):**

Describe a situation in which you regulated (turned up) a positive emotion. Include information about where you were, when it happened, and the circumstances surrounding the event.

_____

_____

_____

1. Where in your body did you feel this emotion?

2. List three words to describe the emotion:

_____

_____

_____

3. What helped you remember to regulate the emotion?

4. What actions did you take to regulate the emotion?

5. Rate how you regulated the emotion (not well; somewhat well; quite well; very well).

6. How did the other person respond (not well; somewhat well; quite well; very well)?

**Negative Emotion (angry; depressed/sad; fearful/anxious; disgusted/contemptuous):**

Describe a situation in which you regulated (turned down) a negative emotion. Include information about where you were, when it happened, and the circumstances surrounding the event.

_____

_____

_____

7. Where in your body did you feel this emotion?

8. List three words to describe the emotion:

_____

_____

_____

9. What helped you remember to regulate the emotion?

10. What actions did you take to regulate the emotion?

11. Rate how you regulated this emotion (not well; somewhat well; quite well; very well).

12. How did the other person respond (not well; somewhat well; quite well; very well)?

# Chapter Five

# I Walk the Line

P arents tell us that discipline tops the list of issues that keep them up nights ruminating about whether they are too strict or too lenient with their children. For this reason, some parents will turn to this chapter first. If you are one of them, turn back to chapter one now, please. If you actually read chapters one through four, in that order, give yourself a token. You are ready to go.

To keep children safe and behaving responsibly, we have to teach them to live in a world full of rules and regulations. As parents, we establish rules and limits that fit our values, and we encourage our children to follow them. Children break rules for all kinds of reasons, and when they do, parents must discipline them. Most of us approach discipline with mixed feelings, which often depend on how your parents disciplined you as a child. One thing we have in common is that, when children break our rules or misbehave, we become upset. Sometimes we overreact. Or, in fear of overreaction, we withdraw and do nothing. If we don't know what to do, we may pretend we don't see what's going on and let important teaching opportunities slip by. To teach children to follow the rules, we have to provide negative consequences when they break them. This means that we have to say "no" sometimes, and then we must stand by our decision.

When you set limits, your children may resort to a full bag of tricks to make you give in. Sometimes they may sweet talk you or become little lawyers; at other times, they may whine, shout, slam doors, or even ply you with guilt. Then, of course, there is the full-blown tantrum. When your children are emotional and push your buttons, you are at high risk for reacting without thinking. Reacting when you are upset fans the flames of conflict. When you set limits, it is vital to be calm, cool, and collected. You also need to be armed with a good plan so that, when confrontations arise, you know just what to do. When your children learn that you have a plan and you mean business, they will come to realize that they may as well get the discipline over.

Somehow, people have come to believe that negative consequences have to be strong and long. Our research shows that effective discipline can be relatively mild and short when used consistently. Thus, our discipline strategies emphasize brevity. Consistency is what counts. When sanctions are small and inevitable, children learn to accept them. And parents are willing to use them.

The most effective negative consequences for rule violations and misbehavior are time outs, disciplinary chores, and privilege loss. Time outs (never exceeding ten minutes) are effective for young children. Disciplinary chores are better suited for older children, although they are appropriate for school-age children as well. Privilege loss serves as an effective backup to enforce time outs and disciplinary chores. The principles behind these negative consequences are the same for all ages—mild, short, consistent, and delivered in a calm yet firm manner. Negative sanctions work best in balance with encouragement for positive behaviors. Cooperation flourishes when you are able to set limits *and* maintain a positive and trusting relationship with your children.

In general, a consequence should be small enough that the parent is willing and able to use it. At the same time, it must be strong enough for your child to consider the cost of disobeying. Below are the elements of any good discipline. Throughout the chapter, we'll show you how to use these different elements depending on the situation.

## Elements of Effective Discipline

- ☑ Small—short and not painful
- ☑ Immediate
- ☑ Consistent
- ☑ Contingent—based on the child's behavior, not your mood
- ☑ Calm and neutral
- ☑ When it's over, let it go and move forward
- ☑ Balanced with encouragement in a 5-to-1 ratio—catch your child being good five times for each negative sanction.

# Time Outs

Nearly fifty years ago, Jerry and a small group of family psychologists developed the use of time outs with children. Since then, time outs have become one of the most widely used (and misused) forms of discipline. In our early attempts to design the procedure, we made time outs too long and didn't have a backup procedure for refusal. I remember a horrendous scene with my son that escalated into a shouting match and a forty-seven-minute time out! I'm not sure who was punished more. Effective discipline is short so that parents and children can accept it and move on. One reason time outs work so well is that they give people a chance to disengage from escalating power struggles.

Most children refuse time outs at some point. When kids won't cooperate with the discipline, both parents and kids forfeit control of the situation. When parents attempt to regain power, they often resort to coercion—they may shout, forcibly drag the child, or make exaggerated threats. *Let it be said loud and clear that none of these approaches reduces coercion or increases cooperation.* You have to have a backup plan for these occasions. Privilege loss is probably the next best step. As is true for all discipline strategies, the loss of privilege should be short. We'll talk more about this later.

Properly executed, time outs look breathtakingly simple. We can assure you, they are not—at least, not at first. Once you learn to use all the elements of a successful time out, however, it will become second nature. Do *not* attempt to use time outs until you have practiced and become comfortable with the technique. It may even be best to forget everything you've ever heard before about time outs and try our technique first. Make sure you follow the steps exactly. Let's start with time outs for school-age children. Later, we will describe how to apply the technique to tiny tots.

## *Strategies for Time Outs*

- Label the behavior that earned the discipline.

- Give your child a clear direction to go to the location you have specified for time outs for five minutes.

- Silently stand and hold for ten seconds.

- Be calm and firm.

- Maintain a neutral expression.

- If your child complies, set your timer for five minutes.

- If your child does not comply, add one minute every three seconds as you continue to stand and hold.

- When you reach ten minutes, tell your child to go to the time-out spot *now* or lose a privilege.

- If your child complies, set the timer for ten minutes. If not, enforce the privilege loss and disengage quickly. Do not argue or discuss.

- When it's over, let it go.

Before using time outs, you have to identify a location where your child will go and stay. Think carefully about this place. It must be *safe* and it must be *boring*. We recently asked our nine-year-old grandson what he thinks about time outs. He quickly responded: "They're boring."

## Strategies for Choosing a Time-Out Spot

- Choose somewhere boring.

- Choose somewhere safe.

- Choose a place away from attention.

- Choose somewhere where you can monitor, but disengage.

- Prepare the area by removing fragile, dangerous, distracting, or entertaining things.

- Identify two or more locations for multiple children.

As you select these locations, take different things into consideration. Think first about safety. The place should not be frightening, closed-in (no closets, please), uncomfortable, or humiliating. Children's bedrooms seldom work if that's where they keep fun stuff like computers, books, toys, and notebooks. Some people use the bathroom. That can be a problem if you have a house full of people and only one bathroom, and it can pose a safety risk if you keep cleaners or medicines in a bathroom cabinet. Some use a laundry room, hallway, or mudroom. Still others use a chair that is somewhat separate from family activity (it does not have to face the wall).

Choose a spot that is appropriate for your individual child's age, personality, and level of functioning. The purpose is disengagement—removal from engaging social settings and separation from interesting things. If you have two or more children, make sure you have selected two or more spots. Depending on the spot and the child's temperament, you may have to remove things that are dangerous, valuable, or fragile. It's better to be safe than sorry, especially while you and your children are learning to use this technique. Some children throw a full-fledged tantrum their first time or two. If you keep checking in on them, however, you are just giving them attention, which is the opposite of your goal. If you are worried about something getting broken, you are giving them attention as well. Essentially, you need to "childproof" the space. Once you and your children are comfortable with the procedure, you can return things to their natural state.

To become adept at the time-out technique, we recommend that you practice with a partner or friend, in front of a mirror, on the subway, in your car, or in the shower. Simply say your child's name, state the problem behavior, and direct your child to go to his or her time-out spot now for five minutes. Do not add words or rationales: "You know you're supposed to do as I say. Why don't you just do it? Now I have to send you to time out." It's ever so tempting, but your child is not interested in your rationale during a confrontation. Save them for times when people, especially you, are calm. In fact, one purpose of the time-out technique was to give a parent time to calm down as well as to discipline the child. It turns out to be effective for both purposes.

We recommend ten minutes maximum for children five and older. For preschoolers, we use one minute per year of age of the child. We do *not* advocate using force or physical restraint to get a child to the time-out spot (as some "experts" do, to our dismay). Our stand-and-hold approach encourages cooperation and provides children with an opportunity to make good choices. They can choose to follow your directions and earn encouragement. Or they can choose not to follow your directions and earn a time out.

Some parents find it helps to use a standard script that reminds them what to say. Some post this in a convenient spot, put it on an index card, or even program it into their phones. Here's a model you can use.

## Time-Out Script

*"[Name], do _____ now, please."* Stand and hold for ten seconds.

If the child doesn't comply, say: *"[Name], do _____ now, please or go to time out for five minutes."* Hold for ten seconds.

If the child still doesn't comply, say: *"That's not following directions. Go to time out for five minutes."* Stand and hold for about three seconds.

If the child does not go, add one minute. *"That's six minutes in time out."* Stand and hold for three seconds.

If the child argues or continues to refuse, add one minute at a time up to ten at three-second intervals. *"That's seven minutes,"* and so on.

At ten minutes, if the child continues to refuse, say: *"Go to time out for ten minutes now or no _____ from ___ to ____."* Stand and hold for three seconds.

If the child continues to refuse, say: *"OK, no _____ from ____ to ____."*

Walk away. Do not discuss.

---

As we mentioned earlier, most children will test the system, so you need a backup strategy for time outs. A good consequence for refusing to cooperate is loss of privilege. This sanction is stronger than a time out, but it is still relatively short, small, and effective. When you start to use time outs, you can bet that, when you have completed the sequence and announced a loss of privilege, your child will try to negotiate and say: "Okay, okay. I'll go to time-out." Although some parents don't follow through with the privilege loss, we advise against this. You want your children to take you at your word. The time out procedure provides children with plenty of chances to cooperate, and yet they may choose not to comply. When you are consistent with your plan and have clearly explained it to your children, you will be surprised how quickly they learn to follow your directions. Children are rational. Following through and being consistent is an important step in building the cooperative spirit you are seeking.

## Time Outs in Action

For most families, dinnertime presents abundant opportunities to practice disciplinary skills. Here's an example of the time-out technique in action.

Robert and Juliette have a nine-year-old son, Jacob, whose favorite new pastime is to Skype with his best friend, who recently moved halfway across the country. As dinner was finishing up, Jacob shoveled down the last of his vegetables and, in a blink, was gone from the table. Robert glanced at his wife and said: "I guess it's my turn?" Juliette smiled and nodded yes. As Robert approached the study, Jacob was already deeply into conversation with his buddy. Robert walked over to the computer and bent down so he appeared on the Skype screen. "Hi, Zach. Jacob will have to get back to you."

Then he turned to Jacob and calmly said: "Jacob, you were not excused from the table. Log off now, please, and come back to the table."

Jacob waved off his father as if he were shooing the cat out of the room, which wasn't the wisest response. Robert calmly leaned into the screen and said: "Bye, Zach," and disconnected the call.

Jacob objected: "Dad! That's rude! We were Skyping!"

Staying cool and controlled, Robert replied: "Jacob, you left the table without being excused, and you dissed me when I told you to come back to the table. That's not following directions. Go to time-out now for five minutes."

Jacob glared at his dad. "No!"

"That's six minutes."

"I hate you!"

Robert added minutes as if there were a metronome ticking in his head: "That's seven minutes."

Jacob was about to yell again, but stopped himself and walked out of the study to sit at the foot of the stairs. Robert returned to the dinner table. Juliette smiled and said: "Congratulations."

· · ·

That situation ended without much pain. Robert did an outstanding job of keeping his cool with his antagonistic son. Jacob had learned from past experience that, once his parents started down the time-out track, they followed it all the way. But what do you do when your child pushes the limits?

"Jacob, that's seven minutes."

"I don't care!"

"Eight minutes," Robert replies, maintaining his poise.

"I said I don't care!"

"Nine minutes."

Jacob ignores his dad and stares at the wall. When another three seconds passes, Robert brings out the heavy artillery.

"Go to time out now for ten minutes or no screen time for thirty minutes. That means no computers, video games, iPad, or TV."

At this point, children will either comply or they won't. If you have followed through before with a loss of privilege, there's a good chance they will choose the ten minutes in time out. After all, that is the rational choice—ten minutes or thirty minutes. If not, they may parry with this classic plea: "Okay, okay. I'm sorry. I won't do it again. I'll go back to the table now and ask to be excused." If you want to be taken seriously, you have to hold your ground. Your child gives up the option to return to the starting point with the first "no."

Let's say Jacob refuses the ten-minute time out.

 Robert says: "Okay, Jacob. No time out. Instead, you lose your screen and tech privileges for thirty minutes, starting now." Then Robert sets the timer on his watch.

• • •

What if Jacob ignores his dad and goes back to the table to play nice?

 "Okay, I'm at the table," Jacob says, piling on the charm. "May I be excused now, please?"

Robert and Juliette hold firm. Robert replies: "Yes, Jacob, you may be excused from the table. But you may not Skype or use any tech for the next thirty minutes." Jacob quietly leaves the table, putting his plate in the sink. Robert sets his timer.

• • •

Maintaining your cool during time-out episodes can be the hardest part of parenting. Most children know exactly how to trigger your sarcasm. When you give them the expected reaction, you reward them for engaging in dead-end exchanges. For a mini-exercise, imagine yourself in

Robert's shoes in the above scenario and think how you might play out the same situation. Then imagine how Jacob would respond. Can you maintain your cool and simply follow the script?

When a disciplinary event is over, it is over. The child broke a rule or misbehaved; the parent gave a consequence; the child paid the price. It serves no good purpose to raise the issue again. The day can move forward with a clean slate. Some parents insist on an apology as the child comes out of the discipline given. In many families, this starts a new episode of misbehavior. Your child may refuse to apologize or do so insincerely, and you may not be satisfied. Now you have a new behavioral situation on your hands. Do not demand an apology. Let the incident go and don't bring it up again. The next time misbehavior takes place, simply use the time-out technique again. After a while, the need for them will decrease. And remember to stay alert to opportunities to catch your child being good so you can rebuild that five-to-one balance of positive to negative.

## Time Out for Tiny Tots

There is a slight variation in the time-out technique for children under five. It follows the same principles, but the time is shortened. One rule of thumb is to start with one minute of discipline for each year of age, up to five. Then add only up to three additional minutes to the original time. So for a three-year-old, start with three minutes, with the possibility of adding up to three more. At six minutes, shift to privilege loss. You may have to walk some preschoolers to the time-out spot, at least at first. Never drag them, however, and avoid talking along the way. Stay calm and be firm, not emotional. Here's how Isabelle and Kayla used time out.

Since the last time we saw them, Isabelle has been earning tokens for following her parents' clear directions. Isabelle knows how to count to ten; when she earns ten tokens, she gets to reach into the grab bag her parents keep stocked with tiny treats. Her parents' new skill at giving clear directions and their use of tokens has helped Isabelle control her "No. Why?" habit. Her parents recently started using time outs, and her tantrums have begun to fade away. She still doesn't like to be told "no," but now she earns a token when she is able to accept it. When her little face clouds up, her mom or dad remind her that, if she accepts the "no" and moves on, she can take a token. Most of the time, that works. When it doesn't, they use a time out. Here's an example of a typical exchange.

"Mommy, can I have a cookie?" Isabelle asks.

"No, sweetie," Kayla replies. "We're going to have supper pretty soon. It will spoil your appetite."

"But Mommy, why can't I have a cookie? I'm hungry now. Just one little cookie, please? It won't spoil me."

Kayla can see a situation developing, so she stands firm: "Isabelle, the answer is 'no.' I'll get you a nice cool glass of water. That'll help you wait. And you can have a token if you stop asking now."

Isabelle refuses the bait: "Nooooooooooooo. Why can't I have a cookie? I want a cookie. Now . . ."

Kayla is ready, however: "Oops. That's not cooperating. That's three minutes in time out. Let's go over to the time-out chair now."

Isabelle stamps her little foot and shouts: "Noooooo!"

Calmly, yet in a firm voice, Kayla responds: "That's now four minutes in time out." She puts out her hand to guide Izzy to the chair.

"No, no, nooooooooooooo."

Kayla calmly says: "That's five minutes."

Isabelle starts to cry.

"Isabelle, that's six minutes now or no dessert." She reaches out her hand.

Isabelle takes her mother's hand and, while crying, walks over to the time-out chair and sits down.

Kayla sets the timer on her phone for six minutes and goes about her work. When the timer goes off, she goes over to Izzy and says: "Okay, Isabelle. Time out is over."

Isabelle comes back with: "I don't care. I'm going to stay here."

Kayla just keeps her cool and says: "Okay. That's your choice." Then she returns to her work.

• • •

Following the structured time-out procedure protects you from falling into old habits in which you react to your children rather than taking charge of the situation. Follow the technique to the letter. Once you have made it second nature, you and your children will be able to recover quickly from disciplinary encounters. You will be tempted to break the routine and do one of many things—lose your temper, give in, argue, provide rationales, move directly to privilege loss, or make threats. Each parent has his or her own special weaknesses and style of dealing with disciplinary confrontations. Anticipate yours and prepare yourself to stand strong.

## Setting Expectations

Before you begin using time outs, tell your children exactly what to expect. When they know how to follow the procedure, they are less anxious and more cooperative. During your explanation, practice how it works. If you have been following a different, less effective form of time out, try our technique, but first explain (and practice) this new approach.

Here is our strategy for explaining the technique to your children.

## *Explaining Time Outs*

- ☑ Because cooperation is important, I'm going to help you remember.

- ☑ When you follow directions, you earn a token.

- ☑ When you don't follow directions, you go to time out.

- ☑ Time out means you go to [specify the time-out spot] for five minutes.

- ☑ If you go right away, the time out will last five minutes.

- ☑ If you don't go or if you argue, I will add one minute at a time.

- ☑ When we get to ten minutes, you lose a privilege, but you don't go to time out.

- ☑ When the time out or privilege loss is over, we're done with the problem.

- ☑ Let's practice how it works.

At first, use time outs only at home and when people are not in a hurry. Once everyone is well rehearsed, you can take the technique with you to the homes of family and friends. Here's an example of how that can work—or not work.

 When Amanda visited her parents, the kids got to play with their grandparents' Wii game. Eight-year-old Jack took the box containing the Wii console, ran to the adjoining TV room with his sister, hooked up the game, and explained the simple rules. Amanda and Grandma could hear the kids playing and everything seemed to be fine.

Meanwhile, Jack was swinging his plastic control, which mimicked the action of a tennis racket, closer and closer to six-year-old Emily's head. Finally, he could no longer resist the temptation. He gently whacked his sister on the back of her head as he pretended to swing at the tennis ball on the screen. In the other room, Amanda heard Jack's belly laugh as Emily let out an exaggerated scream.

"Ow! That hurt, stupid! You did that on purpose!"

"Don't be such a baby," Jack said, still laughing. "You know that didn't hurt."

"OW!! You hit me again, dum-dum!" Emily yelled.

Amanda shook her head, took off down the hall, and grabbed the control from Jack's hand.

"It was an accident, Mom!" Jack whined.

"That's enough! I've had it with both of you," Amanda shouted. "Give me those controls! No more Wii for the rest of the day. Jack, you know better than to hit your sister. Go to the guest room and stay in time out until I say you can come out. Emily, you know better than to call your brother names. You go to time out in Grandma's room and stay there as long as I say!"

Both children started crying and pleaded not to go into perpetual time out. For the next half hour, the children cried and begged to come out, constantly interrupting Amanda's conversation with her mom. Finally, they wore Amanda down and she relented.

• • •

Let's evaluate how well Amanda followed the time-out technique in this difficult situation, starting with what she did well. Amanda intervened quickly, which prevented the children from escalating further. The consequence was immediate. She wisely did not take sides—each child got the same consequence. Those are the things Amanda did well.

Where were the errors? The consequence was neither short nor clearly defined. Remember, the steps call for sending each child to time out, starting with five minutes and adding one minute at a time until reaching ten minutes. She also took away Wii privileges for the rest of the day. By making the punishment too long and too strong, she punished herself and her mother as well, and she finally fell into the coercion trap by giving in to her children's pleas. Let's rewind and give her another chance.

 When she pulled out the Wii, Amanda reminded her children of the rules for cooperative play: follow the rules, use polite language, and keep your hands and feet to yourself. She also consulted with her mother about possible time-out spots, just in case. The family had been using time outs at home for months, so both children knew what to do.

Hearing the argument escalate, Amanda intervened: "That's enough! Stop right now!" She stood in the doorway, hands on her hips, breathing deeply. Because she had a plan, and especially because she was well-practiced, the children looked at her and at each other, pretty much knowing what was about to happen.

"Both of you will now have time out for not following the rules for cooperative play. Jack, you go to the guest room; Emily, you go to Grandma's room. Go now, each of you, for five minutes."

Emily protested: But it was his fault!"

"She called me names!" Jack countered.

Amanda held firm: "That's six minutes."

Resigned, both children got up and marched silently to their separate spots. And peace returned to the realm.

. . .

Practice this technique at home and have it letter-perfect before you take it on the road. Parents who skip the home practice consistently report failure. This is a skill for everyone in the family—parents and children.

# Privilege Loss

Time outs will not work without a powerful backup to use when your children refuse to comply. Most children will refuse on occasion—some more than others, and some more vehemently. Privilege loss is a negative consequence in which youngsters lose access to something they value for a designated period of time. Privileges that you remove should *not* be incentives that your children have earned.

## *Strategies for Revoking Privileges*

☐ Make it short—fifteen to thirty minutes.

☐ Make it longer and stronger than ten minutes in time out.

☐ Revoke the privilege shortly after the refusal to comply.

☐ Be willing and able to withhold this privilege.

☐ Make sure the privilege loss doesn't punish parents or other family members.

☐ Choose something you can control without a struggle.

☐ Choose a privilege that has value to your child.

As always, plan ahead. You'll feel like a fool if you are in the midst of the time-out procedure, get to the privilege loss step, and can't think of a privilege to withhold. Have a list of several potential privileges ready. Different circumstances dictate different choices. Many parents escalate quickly into longer and stronger consequences. But remember the guidelines—keep it small; keep it fair; be consistent. While making your privilege list, be sure that you can actually control the privilege that you're going to remove. Ask yourself if its removal will punish you or others. If the loss is too large, you put yourself at risk for giving in. Make sure the loss has value to your child. Try to anticipate any problems that may arise. As angry as you may feel when one of your children misbehaves, you really don't want to be mean or unfair. Here are a few suggestions for privileges you can revoke.

## Examples of Privileges

### Entertainment

- ☑ Screen time
- ☑ Video games
- ☑ TV

### Social Activities

- ☑ Playing outside
- ☑ Having a friend over
- ☑ Going to a friend's house
- ☑ Texting
- ☑ Phone

**Treats**

- ☑ Dessert

- ☑ Special snacks

Engage your children in making a list of potential privileges to remove. You can build buy-in if you allow them to participate in the choice of options. Make sure the list reflects your children's ages and interests.

# Disciplinary Chores

By about age ten or eleven, time outs become less effective. When that day arrives, move straight to disciplinary chores. A disciplinary chore is an extra job that you assign as a negative consequence for misbehavior or rule violations. Examples include sweeping the front porch and sidewalk, pulling weeds, shoveling snow, scrubbing the bathtub, stacking wood, or vacuuming the living room. Young children can do chores as well. Our grandchild began doing them around age five. Keep it simple for little children; older children can do more complex jobs.

The length and type of a disciplinary chore depends on the age and skills of the child and the behavior that earned the consequence. Short chores, which should be used for small infractions or with younger children, can be completed at a reasonable pace in five to ten minutes. When you assign a chore, clearly spell out the detailed expectations of the job. When our children were young, we used a woodstove for heat, so we had lots of firewood in need of splitting and stacking. As an adult, one of our sons told us that he used to weigh the pleasure of indulging in a rule violation with the pain of stacking wood. In a sense, he chose, knowing there would be a specific cost for his behavior.

Like all disciplinary tools, a chore is not revenge. It is a mild negative consequence designed to discourage specific misbehavior or rule violations. When considering how long a job should take, be generous. If you can do the job in five minutes, assume it will take your child ten minutes. If the job is finished properly before that time, you have a win-win situation.

Just as you discussed with your children how time outs would work, hold a meeting and explain when and how disciplinary chores will be used. Prepare a menu of chores so your children know what to expect as a consequence for specific behaviors. Remember that they are children, however; set them up to be successful. Before you assign a chore, write up a job description and teach them how to do it.

Here are the steps for building a successful disciplinary chore routine.

## Strategies for Disciplinary Chores

- Make a list of privileges that can be withheld until a chore is completed.

- Make a list of potential chores.

- Begin with brief chores that can be completed in five minutes.

- Write job descriptions (on index cards or as apps) for specific chores.

- Calmly state the rule violation or misbehavior that earned the chore.

- Calmly state the privilege that will be withheld until the chore is completed.

- Calmly present the chore's job description.

- Do not lecture, argue, or discuss after assigning the chore.

- Disengage while the chore is being completed.

- Review the job; make sure it fulfills the details of the job description.

- If the chore is incomplete, calmly state what is done well and what remains to be done.

- When the job is done, the matter is over.

- Restore the privilege that was withheld during the discipline.

Disciplinary chores can be anything useful that falls outside your child's normal routine. The length of time required to complete the chore should be commensurate with the severity of the misbehavior. Shorter chores—for minor infractions and younger children—will normally take from five to fifteen minutes to complete. Longer chores—for more serious misdemeanors or for older children—can take from thirty minutes to an hour.

Disciplinary chores should be extras; they serve as negative consequences. Some families make this distinction by calling them extra chores. They are the jobs that nobody likes to do, but that must be done—like scrubbing the toilet bowl. They should not be mean-spirited or dangerous, however, and they should be easy for your children to accomplish. Do not include your children's regular chores. Always start with short and simple chores. That way, everyone can learn the process and get used to it. Your children can graduate to more complicated jobs as they mature and become more skillful. Once, I gave my son the job of trimming the bushes around my roses. That was the end of my roses!

Pages 142 and 143 describe some sample chores you can use to start your own list. Choose those that are appropriate for your family, then add more of your own.

## Short Chores—5 to 15 minutes

☑ Clean the kitchen sink

☑ Sweep the floor

☑ Clean the toilet bowl

☑ Clean out a kitchen cabinet

☑ Clean the bathroom sink

☑ Empty the dishwasher

☑ Pooper-scooper patrol in the yard

☑ Fold one load of laundry

☑ Dust one room

☑ Vacuum the carpet in one room

☑ Wipe down one wall

☑ Sweep the sidewalk

☑ Clean the tub or shower

☑ Clean out the refrigerator

☑ Scrub the floor

☑ Clean the mirror in the bathroom

☑ Sort the recycling box

☑ Clean out the garbage can

☑ Bring in firewood

☑ Sweep out the garage

## Long Chores—30 minutes to 1 hour

- ☑ Clean mold off the tiles in the shower
- ☑ Wash windows
- ☑ Scrub the outside of pots and pans
- ☑ Rake leaves
- ☑ Clean mold off windows
- ☑ Pull weeds
- ☑ Wash down sections of the outside of the house
- ☑ Chop wood and/or stack it
- ☑ Detail the inside of the car
- ☑ Mow the lawn; rake it
- ☑ Clean out and sort the recycling area
- ☑ Edge the grass
- ☑ Clean the oven
- ☑ Scrub the car wheels
- ☑ Clean an area of the garage

Creating detailed job descriptions for your disciplinary chores is an important step in the process. Without a clear description of your expectations, your children may have a hard time completing the chore to your satisfaction. They may also take advantage of no description by setting their own expectations for the task at hand. Here is a sample job description for cleaning the cat litter box.

## Sample Job Description

**Chore: Cleaning the cat litter box**

1. Empty the litter into specified space.

2. Hose out the litter box.

3. Add soap.

4. Scrub the litter box with cat-litter scrub brush.

5. Hose out box to rinse.

6. Dry with paper towels.

7. Add litter to the mark in the box.

8. Return the litter box to the appropriate place (laundry room).

9. Clean up all spilled litter.

10. Return the scrub brush to the proper place (bottom shelf in garage).

11. Wash your hands.


## Disciplinary Chores in Action

Here's how one mother used the disciplinary chore technique with her own children, and with a neighbor boy as well.

Tara is a single mother raising a twelve-year-old son, Kyle, and a nine-year-old daughter, Janelle. She introduced time outs to her children at about the time Kyle entered kindergarten and Janelle was a toddler. "The technique works well with both children for behaviors that are in your face—things like not following directions, talking back, or arguing with each other," Tara said. She was good at noticing their voices rising in the family room. When she intervened, each child would blame the other for the problem. "It was futile to try and figure out who was to blame," she observed, "so I just sent both of them to their time-out spots. That broke up the fight and they were able to come back and play again. Sometimes I had to take away a privilege, but usually it was my fault. I just waited too long before stepping in, and they got so riled up that there was no stopping them." When Tara needed something else to deal with other kinds of behaviors—things like rule-breaking, coming home late, and destructive activities—she discovered the value of chores.

 One afternoon as she pulled into her driveway, Tara was astonished to see that a large portion of it was covered with sparkling silver paint. As the concrete glistened in the afternoon sun, Tara spied Kyle, Janelle, and the neighbor's boy trying to ditch several empty spray-paint cans. Tara was ready to scream. She knew there was no way anyone could scrub that paint off. She wasn't sure what to do, so she drove down the street, parked, and listened to some music to cool off. She decided to use chores as a disciplinary strategy. She returned home and maintained a neutral expression as she stepped from the car. "The kids could tell they were in trouble," she explained, "so what purpose would it serve to come out yelling like a crazy woman?" Hands on her hips, she calmly surveyed the kids' handiwork, nodding her head.

"The kids had found the paint in the garage and one thing led to another. I told them the driveway was not a canvas for their artistic expression and the consequences would be immediate chores, one for each. You should have seen the surprise on their faces. I gave each of them an hour of doing something they did not want to do. I told my son to mow the front yard while Janelle and the neighbor's boy pulled weeds. My driveway was a mess, but my yard was a thing of beauty! When they finished their jobs, I let it go and that was that. I spoke to the neighbor boy's mother, and she decided she was going to try these disciplinary chores out herself."

• • •

This next scenario describes using the disciplinary chores with a young school-age child.

Andy had begged for a dog since he was old enough to talk. With his seventh birthday approaching, his parents, Paul and Sarah, agreed it was time. They believed having a dog would be a great way to teach Andy new responsibilities. The basic tasks of brushing the dog's coat, picking up chew toys, and filling the water bowl would provide easy routine chores. Paul and Sarah used an incentive chart to help Andy learn his new responsibilities. The weekend before his birthday, the family drove to the shelter to pick out their newest family member—a two-month-old Spaniel mix. Andy beamed on the way home and announced he was naming the dog Sparky because he had sparkly eyes.

The first few weeks went almost perfectly. Andy dutifully kept Sparky's water dish full, and he spent hours each day playing with the dog in the house and outside in the family's fenced yard. Seeing that the match was working out, Paul enrolled Sparky in training classes to learn basic commands and how to walk on a leash. Andy attended the puppy classes with his dad and learned to give treats when Sparky obeyed the commands.

"Hey, Dad. It's kind of like tokens for Sparky," Andy giggled.

"Well, I suppose we all deserve to be rewarded when we learn new things," Paul said with a smile.

The part of puppy training that Andy did not understand well was discipline. Paul and Sarah were tidying the kitchen after dinner one evening when they heard a series of frightened yelps come from Andy's bedroom. Sarah ran down the hall to investigate. She opened the door and saw Andy shaking a badly chewed action figure at Sparky.

"No, Sparky! Bad dog," Andy yelled as he hit Sparky over the head with a mangled Superman. Sparky yelped again as Sarah rushed into the room.

"Andy! Stop it," Sarah interrupted. "You're hurting him."

Andy started crying: "See what Sparky did to Superman." He was about to smack the dog again when Sarah caught his raised arm. She took the toy from Andy and picked up Sparky. She took a few seconds to compose herself and also to soothe the frightened animal.

"Andy, we don't ever hit Sparky. You could have hurt him and you've scared him half to death," Sarah said. She checked Sparky to ensure that Andy had not inflicted any serious damage. "You wouldn't want me or Daddy to hit you like that, would you?"

"No." Andy stared at the floor and squirmed.

"Animals have feelings too and they feel pain just like we do," Sarah explained.

"I don't care!" Andy said.

Sarah remained quiet and considered what to do next. When Paul walked into the room, Sarah whispered: "Your turn."

Andy asked: "Do I have to go to time out now?"

"No," his dad answered. "This is really serious, Andy. Instead of time out, you will have to do a chore. I think the proper chore should be something you don't like doing and I know what that should be."

"What?" Andy asked nervously.

"You have 'pooper-scooper' patrol." Paul calmly led Andy to the back porch where they kept the tools for the job nobody liked. He showed Andy exactly what was expected. Then Paul sat down and watched Andy complete the job. When he was done, Paul looked about and praised him for his good work. They high-fived and went back inside.

The next day, Paul explained that hitting or kicking Sparky causes pain and that pulling the dog's tail or pulling hard on his leash can also cause pain. Paul then explained that, whenever Andy did something to hurt Sparky, he would have another extra chore.

. . .

Paul and Sarah used a beautiful combination of teaching skills: encouraging positive behavior with tokens and discouraging problem behavior with chores. You can use time outs for small face-to-face misbehavior (like noncompliance). But other problems—hurting others (adults, children, and pets), lying, cheating, intentional property destruction, and stealing—need a stiffer consequence. The principles for both forms of discipline follow the general rules: keep it short; make it immediate; use few words; and when the time is served or the task completed, the situation is over—no further discussion is needed. Notice that Andy got his consequence immediately and without a long lecture on the meaning of inflicting pain. His parents wisely waited until the next day to have that conversation, making it more likely that Andy would hear their message.

## Lengthy Disciplinary Chores

Sometimes a five- or ten-minute—or even a thirty-minute—chore is not a strong enough sanction given the nature of the misdeed. Dangerous, serious, and otherwise ugly situations may call for an extended chore that lasts a couple of hours or more. That requires a little tweaking of the technique. Practice with short chores before using this technique to impose lengthy ones. To begin, follow the disciplinary chore technique given above. Then make the following adjstments.

## Strategies for Lengthy Disciplinary Chores

- Decide how long the chore should be to pay for the violation.

- If money is involved, establish a rate of pay. Be generous; the goal is success.

- Select specific chores from your list.

- Provide relevant job descriptions.

- Specify a reasonable amount of time for the youngster to spend doing chore(s) each day, or determine what chores must be completed on a given day. An hour or two per day is best, depending on the child.

- Determine when during the day the chore will be done.

- At the appointed time, begin withholding the relevant privilege until the chore or allotted time is completed.

- Review the job; make sure it fulfills the details of the job description.

- When the chore is completed, restore the privilege.

Stealing is a good example of a behavior that requires a stiffer penalty. The next scenario provides an example of dealing with an older child who engaged in stealing.

After Cloe's thirteenth birthday, her mom, Jessica, began letting her spend part of her allowance on makeup. When shopping for essentials at the store, Jessica allowed her to hang out in the makeup section, where she could spend her own money on inexpensive mascara or foundation. On occasion, Jessica let Chloe apply her own makeup under her watchful eye. The house rule was that she was never to use her mom's makeup.

Suffice it to say that a new crush on a boy was enough to make Chloe temporarily lose her sanity one morning before school. Jessica had already left for work when Chloe realized she had squeezed the last drop from her $6.95 tube of makeup. So Chloe tiptoed into her mom's bathroom, where, in the medicine cabinet, a cornucopia of choices awaited her. With little time to spare before the school bus arrived, Chloe selected a one-ounce bottle of expensive foundation. She reasoned that she would apply it in the bathroom at school before class and return it to her mom's cabinet after school. Since Jessica didn't come home until about six o'clock, she would never know.

At school, Chloe applied a tiny dollop of the foundation. She marveled at how perfectly it covered her blemishes and she loved the smell. So did the girl at the mirror next to her.

"Oh, I love that brand," said the girl. "Mind if I try a little?"

Chloe hesitantly handed the bottle to her. She didn't know her well, but she was very popular. Another girl approached from behind.

"OMG, that is the best. Let me try," said the second girl.

A crowd of girls gathered around Chloe begging to try the makeup. In less than two minutes, the little bottle was empty. Chloe felt a knot form in her stomach. The fear and guilt passed quickly, however, as she went to her classes and flirted with her crush during breaks. When she returned home, she was torn between putting the empty bottle back in the cabinet or throwing it away and hoping her mom wouldn't notice. She decided to chuck it in the outside trash can. A couple of days passed and her mom said nothing. Chloe decided that her mom had so much makeup that she would never miss it. Wrong.

Jessica had a formal presentation to make at work and decided to use her best makeup for the occasion. She searched her bathroom cabinet in vain for the little bottle that cost $45 an ounce, even over the Internet. She had used it just last week. It had to be there, unless it had grown legs and walked off by itself. That wasn't likely, Jessica thought. However, there was another set of legs in the house that might be involved.

"Chloe! Can you come here for a second?"

Chloe felt a familiar knot twist in her stomach as she approached her mother's bathroom. Putting on her sweetest smile, she bounced into the room and gave her mom a quick hug. "Hey, mom! Whoa, you look really nice this morning."

"Chloe, have you seen my special bottle of foundation? It was right here in my cabinet."

"Um, no."

What to do, what to do! Not only had Chloe taken her mother's makeup, but now she lied about it as well. A litigious parent might have further entrapped her daughter. But Jessica prevented her from sinking deeper into the quicksand by saying: "Chloe, I know you took my makeup. You'll only make your situation worse by lying." Chloe confessed. When she tried to make excuses, Jessica stopped her, telling her they would finish the conversation after dinner. She had to go to work, and Chloe had to go to school.

• • •

Disengaging for work and school gave Jessica time to cool off and make a plan of action. Chloe had lots of practice with short chores for non-compliance and talking back. Taking her mother's expensive makeup, however, called for a consequence that was longer and stronger than vacuuming the living room floor. Fortunately, Jessica was prepared. She consulted the lengthy disciplinary chore strategies and made a plan.

Jessica decided that Chloe would have to replace the makeup (at $45 a bottle). She would also have to perform a thirty-minute chore for taking the makeup without permission (some might call it stealing). The lie would cost a fifteen-minute chore. If Chloe worked for her mom at the rate of ten dollars an hour, she would need to work four and a half hours to pay for the makeup. That made for a total of five and a quarter hours of discipline. Clearly, that much work at one time would be too much to ask of a thirteen-year-old. Jessica was willing to have Chloe complete about one hour of work each day, so she could fully compensate her mother in less than one week.

Jessica made a menu of chores for Chloe to complete. She had her detail the inside of her car (ninety minutes) and the outside of her car (ninety minutes), wipe down the insides and outsides of the kitchen cabinets (another ninety minutes), and wash the inside and outside of the garbage can and recycling bin (forty-five minutes). It was easy to select a privilege to withhold—no social communication (phone calls, texting, Skype, or Facebook).

Lengthy disciplinary chores require more effort from parents, as well as more work for children. When you break the job into chunks with daily expectations (one or two hours a day), the project becomes doable. The problem is that the parent must make sure that the child does each day's share—withholding the given privilege until the daily effort is fulfilled. Most children make at least one attempt to skip a daily assignment, but still have access to their privilege. You may be tempted to relent. Be strong. Be calm. Be sympathetic. But be firm.

# Recap

And there you have it. Five decades of research on discipline rolled into one chapter. Recognizing and regulating emotions are particularly important when you have to provide sanctions for painted driveways, temper tantrums, missing makeup, siblings smacking each other, back talk, and children intentionally testing your limits. Establishing new discipline procedures may seem like a lot of work. And it is, at first. But once you and your children become practiced, the cooperative spirit you are seeking will grow and grow. There is one condition, however. You have to maintain that positive-to-negative balance of five to one.

With your foundation firmly established, we are now ready to move forward into some of the relational aspects of parenting. In the next chapter, we'll focus on how to listen to your children in ways that make them feel understood. Before you move on, however, work through the practice assignment so you'll be equipped when you have to use a negative consequence.

## Practice Assignment

Most parents attempt to do too much at once. They decide to institute time outs, privilege loss, and disciplinary chores all at the same time. That is a recipe for failure. Pick *either* time outs or chores and practice one until you and your children can follow the technique comfortably. Once you're good at that, you can move on to another tool. Both time outs and chores require that you have your list of privileges ready and at hand, because neither will work without a good backup. So start by making a list of privileges you can withhold.

☑ Include five or six privileges over which you have complete control. Don't use rewards or incentives your child earns. Anticipate problems you may have in withholding the privilege.

☑ Decide whether to start with time outs or disciplinary chores. Carefully prepare for the one you choose, following the techniques given above.

☑ Continue practicing giving clear directions.

☑ Continue using your encouragement systems. In fact, up your pace. When you start focusing on discipline, you want to be sure that you are especially effective at shining the light on the positive behaviors you want to grow.

## Implementing Time Outs

☑ Choose a spot that is dull, boring, and safe. Remove dangerous, valuable, or fragile items.

☑ Introduce time outs to your children. If you have been using another form of time out, explain that you're changing the procedure. This is the new way.

☑ Practice the time-out script in your head—while you're showering, driving, or riding the subway. Practice with an adult.

☑ Use time outs at home before taking them out on the road.

☑ Use them early in the chain of events and *stay calm*.

☑ Take note of your successes and congratulate yourself.

## Implementing Disciplinary Chores

☑ Make a list of potential chores.

☑ Review the sample job description above and then create your own for each chore on your list. Be detailed.

☑ Introduce the disciplinary chore technique to your children.

☑ Practice with an adult.

☑ Start with short chores.

# What Do Parents Say?

When parents lose control or use negative consequences that are long and strong, they feel guilty. That makes it hard for them to be consistent. Because time outs and disciplinary chores are effective, parents have to punish less often. Here's what one parent said.

> *I used to spank my child for any little thing she did. It hurt me to do it because she is my daughter. Now, I use time outs to keep myself calm and that has helped me a lot. No more yelling or spanking. Now, my mind can be calm.*

> *I used to feel bad and so did my son, because I was punishing him all the time. Then I started doing time outs and using disciplinary chores, and it feels so much better. Your families don't train you how to do this.*

Should you make your children apologize for their misdeeds when a time out or a chore is completed? Here are two different views.

> *When time out is over, I want my children to apologize and show that they understand what they did was wrong. I need to know that they know.*

> *When the punishment is over, it's over. Here's what you did; here's*

*the consequence. Tomorrow is a new day. I mean, let's not ruin the whole week.*

Some parents feel that time outs are too strong a punishment. Others feel they are too weak. Because time outs are short, however, kids learn to accept them and parents are willing to use them. Here are two opposing views.

- *Time outs seem like such an insignificant punishment.*

- *Time outs are too strong. They seems like shunning or social isolation.*

Some parents who object to time outs don't have a problem with shouting, name-calling, and making threats. And some fear that using chores as a disciplinary action will teach children to hate work. But chores are a teaching tool, not revenge. They are reasonable and fair. Often, they are jobs nobody likes to do, like cleaning the litter box or scrubbing the toilet bowl. Our own children grew up with disciplinary chores and each one of them is an effective worker.

# Chapter Six

# Stop, Look, Listen

---

This chapter is about *active listening*. With children, you have to listen with all the attention you can muster—even when you're busy, tired, bored, or distracted—if you want to make communications with your children a two-way street.

Communication combines listening and talking. Few people need practice talking. But most of us can improve our listening skills. The better you are able to listen to your children, the more they will confide in you and the closer your relationship will be. To us, communication is like a dance. One person leads (talks), while the other one follows (listens). Then they reverse roles. When you are the listener, your job is to focus on what the other person is saying. With practice, you become better at anticipating your children's responses in the same way that dance partners anticipate each other's moves. Good dance partners cover the floor in synchrony, responding to each other's subtle cues. This chapter will teach you how to do the same with your children by enhancing your communication with them, and even with other adults.

## Nonverbal Messages

As humans, we rely heavily on spoken language. Nonverbal communication is equally important, however. Many times people *say* one thing while sending an entirely different message through their body language, facial expressions, and tone of voice. You may be saying, "I'm so proud that you got an A on the math test," but if you are thinking about something that makes you sad or angry, your body language may reflect that negative emotion. Your child is likely to misinterpret your words as false praise, or—more accurately—assume that you aren't interested or paying attention. So it is important to match your words with your nonverbal language. And that requires that you eliminate other thoughts from your mind and focus your attention on your child. Multitasking is no way to communicate with children. When you show interest in your children, you communicate that you care about them.

Earlier, we talked about regulating emotions. To become an active listener you will draw on those skills. Some of the stories that children tell us trigger emotions and make us angry, anxious, or sad. When we react with negative emotions, our children may stop talking and we miss the opportunity to hear what's going on in their sharp young minds. Parents invite conversation when they follow this simple rule: *Respond; don't react.* Reactions are like reflexes—tap the knee in the right place and it will jerk. Responses require thought. Thinking is what separates a response from a reflexive reaction.

Let's look in on Troy and his family again for an example of this.

 Teri and Alan have watched their son Troy bounce around the house over the past three weeks with unbridled glee. Normally a quiet boy, Troy chatted with his parents during dinner about sports and told funny stories about his friends and teachers. He finished his homework without being told and started asking Teri and Alan for extra chores to earn money for new clothes. Instead of the baggy pants, faded T-shirts, and basketball shoes that had been his uniform since the fifth grade, Troy began asking for plaid shirts, dark jeans, and a pair of Vans to wear to school. One morning, Troy even asked his dad if he could borrow a splash of cologne. "Sure," Alan replied, as

Troy's cheeks flushed red. "Does this have anything to do with a certain girl named Carina?" Troy grinned as Alan gave him a high five.

For two months, life was as perfect as it could be for Troy. Isn't love grand? But eight weeks is a long time for a seventh-grade relationship. One afternoon, Alan came home from work early to change clothes and meet his friends to shoot hoops. This was his "boy's night out." He found Troy slumped on the couch watching reruns of a serial. Troy was dressed in his old baggy camos, a faded green T-shirt, and basketball shoes.

"Hey Troy, what's up?" Alan asked, taking a seat in the recliner next to the couch. He could tell something had happened and suspected it was girl trouble. Troy didn't respond. He held the remote in one hand and a sheet of crumpled pink notepaper in the other. Alan sat in silence for a couple of awkward minutes, unsure what to do next. He needed to leave for the gym, but he felt badly for his son. Troy aimed the remote at the TV screen. It blinked off. He sat up on the couch and turned toward his dad.

"Dad, can we talk about something?" Troy asked.

Without thinking, Alan looked at his watch. He really wanted to be at the gym in half an hour—not enough time to get into a conversation about lost love with a twelve-year-old. Troy was closely watching his dad's body language. Before Alan could reply, Troy said: "Never mind. It ain't no big deal."

"You mean it *isn't* a big deal," Alan said.

"Whatever, Dad," Troy said, getting up from the couch. Alan felt guilt wash over him. He wanted to say something, but this was his one night of the week to be out of the house. For Alan, it was his therapy.

"Listen, buddy, I can tell something's bothering you. So I'm going to get with you tomorrow and we'll work it out, okay?" Alan said, feeling less guilty already.

"Sure, Dad," Troy said from the end of the hallway. Then he slipped into his bedroom and closed the door. When the next morning rolled around, Troy's sadness had turned to anger. Later that day, he ended up in a fight when someone teased him about being dumped by his girlfriend. The fight drew a three-day suspension, which Alan and Teri had to address with discipline at home. Troy's unattended broken heart had transformed quickly into a more serious, complex problem.

• • •

Alan started out well by noticing that his son could use a buddy. He sat down and was ready to give him *some* attention, just as long as it didn't disrupt his plans for the evening. He genuinely wanted to listen, but this was his special night. When Troy asked to talk, Alan looked at his watch, sending a nonverbal message that he didn't have time for him. Even though he promised attention tomorrow, a twelve-year-old in pain feels every moment as an eternity. What a missed opportunity for Alan! Let's rewind and see if there's another way to handle this delicate situation.

 "Dad, can we talk about something?" Troy asked.

Without thinking, Alan looked at his watch. He needed to be at the gym in half an hour—not enough time to get into a conversation about lost pubescent love. But Alan recognized that his son was experiencing the searing, dramatic pain of that first breakup and needed his guidance. He quickly returned his attention to Troy.

"Sure, buddy. Go grab your gym bag and sneakers. You're coming with me."

Troy's eyes lit up, excited at the prospect of spending time with his dad and his dad's friends. He felt special to be included. In the car, Alan said: "Okay, Troy. What do you want to talk about? I'm all ears."

"Carina dumped me, Dad. I feel sick—like my stomach is all twisted inside. I've never felt this bad."

"I'm so sorry, Troy," Alan replied. "What did she say to you?"

"She gave me this note. Can I read it to you?"

Alan noticed that Troy was sitting up straight in the car, holding the same sheet of pink paper. "Go for it."

*"Dear Troy, you are a very nice person, but I will be going to camp and traveling with my family a lot this summer and I think we should be free to meet other people. I wanted you to know that this has nothing to do with you. It's me. I hope we can still be friends. Carina."*

Alan could see that Troy was on the verge of tears. He waited a few seconds to let him pull himself together. "She said that? It's not you, it's me? Can we be friends? Oh man! Well, nothing has changed since I was your age. I've heard that line before, too."

"What does it mean, Dad?" Troy asked.

"It means she's acting like a twelve-year-old."

Troy retorted: "She *is* a twelve-year-old, Dad."

"See? See what I mean?" Alan offered. "You're figuring this out already. Plus, buddy, she's right about one thing for sure. You will be meeting lots of new girls this summer. Woo hoo!"

They both chuckled. Alan reached his arm across the car and gave his son a pat on his back. "Troy, I'm sorry. I know how it hurts when someone breaks up with you. But it's normal and you're going to be all right."

Troy thought about that for a minute, then asked: "Well, how are we supposed to be friends now?"

"Oh, don't worry about that," Alan answered. "That's what girls and boys say. If you're going to be real friends, it will happen by itself. What most kids mean by 'I hope we can friends' is 'I hope you won't think I'm a jerk.' I'm not sure they really understand it either." Alan paused. He saw that Troy was hanging on every word. "At least you got to experience that great feeling when you like someone and they like you back. When you see her at school, just be polite. Don't say bad things about her to your friends. That's the most important thing. Don't let your hurt feelings hurt her feelings. If you can be cool, other girls will see that you are a gentleman, and they will like you even more."

"Okay," Troy agreed. "But I don't think I want to hang out with her anymore."

"That's okay," said Alan, reassuringly. "You have more important things to do now, like shoot some baskets with me and my friends and watch our game. I need you to pay close attention to how I play and, when the game's over, you and I will go out for pizza. Then you can tell me how to play better."

• • •

Alan was able to, as the Beatles once sang, "take a sad song and make it better." The most important thing he did was recognize that his son was hurting and show him that he cared. Take a look at the active listening strategies below and note the ways Alan applied them. Did he stop what he was doing and show his son genuine interest? Noticing that Troy was down in the dumps, he changed his plans to include his son in his night out, which made Troy feel special and took his mind off his pain. Dad's comments normalized the situation, letting Troy know that he, too, had been rejected by girls. Was there a bit of humor in pointing out that she acted like a twelve-year-old? Perhaps the hardest thing for Alan was waiting until he was asked before offering his son advice.

Alan's friends treated Troy like one of them and told funny stories about girls breaking up. By the time they went out for pizza, the feeling of rejection was almost gone. Troy went to bed that night feeling closer to his father and knowing that he was going to be okay. He was able to go to school the next day without being twisted with anxiety. All it took for this small miracle was Dad paying attention and making communication with his son the priority.

## Strategies for Active Listening

Stop, look, and listen. Take a break from whatever you are doing and fully engage. Use positive body language. Show that you care with your non-verbal expressions, with eye contact, and with positive facial expressions.

- ☑ Have a pleasant tone of voice. Sound sincere, interested, and non-negative.

- ☑ Use encouraging words. Focus on the positive and say something nice.

- ☑ Observe your children's expressions. How can you tell what they are feeling? Look at their faces. Listen to their tone of voice. Notice their body language.

- ☑ Put yourself in your children's shoes. See things through their eyes by taking on their age, size, gender, and background experiences.

- ☑ Listen for the message. Hear the story as your child is telling it, without focusing on emotions—the child's or your own.

☑ Paraphrase. Restate what your child is saying using similar words, while focusing on positive, future-oriented thoughts.

☑ Make facilitating comments. Show you're interested with a word here and there—Oh! Hmmm! Really? Wow! Uh oh.

☑ Ask questions about what happened, where and when it happened, and who was involved. To better understand, draw a picture in your mind. Use questions to fill in the scene.

☑ Control your emotions. Your child's story may be upsetting. Worry about it later. Listen with a neutral ear.

☑ Show respect. Provide the same courtesy you like to receive.

☑ If appropriate, ask what, if anything, your child wants from you. Wait until they have finished their story before asking. They may simply want you to listen—accept that. Or they may want advice—if they ask and you have some, offer it!

As with all parenting principles, there are right and wrong ways to respond when your children are trying to tell you something. Here are some traps to avoid.

## Active Listening Don'ts

⊘ Don't interrupt. Listen.

⊘ Don't jump to conclusions. Get the facts.

⊘ Don't focus on the negative. Listen for the positive side of the story.

⊘ Don't become an interrogator. Limit questions and ask them one at a time in an interested, nondemanding manner.

- Don't tell your own story. You can talk about your similar experiences another time.

- Don't give advice until it's asked for. Your advice will be more valuable then.

- Don't try to fix the problem. Set another time to solve problems. Advice and problem-solving come after information-gathering.

- Don't let your emotions interfere. Keep your attention on your child. If you look upset, your child may shut down or exaggerate.

## Things that Go Bump in the Night

We often need to remind ourselves that children's issues are important to them no matter how trivial or silly they may seem to us. One example of this involves children's nighttime terrors. Many children pass through a stage in which they experience some fear of the dark or sleeping in their own rooms. They may try the "boogeyman" tactic to leverage their way into their parents' beds. So when kids start seeing monsters, it's natural to be skeptical. Using the active listening strategies above can help you calm your child at bedtime or in the middle of the night, and prevent you from turning into a monster yourself.

Let's see what happens in one family when the parent doesn't follow the recipe.

Noah is four years old and has been sleeping in his own room with moderate success for the past year or so. Eric and Rachel work at the same hospital—Eric five days a week from 7:00 a.m. to 4:00 p.m. as a nurse practitioner, and Rachel three days a week as an ICU nurse from 6:00 p.m. to 6:00 a.m. Eric has the primary responsibility for putting Noah to bed. Rachel juggles the morning routines and transporting Noah to and from preschool.

The challenges began when Noah started preschool. Eric learned quickly that, when Noah wakes up in the middle of night, so does he. His goal was to have Noah in bed by 7:30 with lights out by 8:15. After helping Noah don his pajamas and brush his teeth, Eric stretched out on the bed and read stories to him for about half an hour. As soon as Noah fell asleep, Eric enjoyed a glass of wine before snoozing in his own bed.

The first week at preschool went pretty smoothly. The monsters arrived the second week. Eric had just drifted off to sleep when he heard Noah crying. He climbed from bed and rushed to Noah's aid. He opened the bedroom door to find him sitting up hugging his pillow.

"Noah, what's wrong? Are you okay?"

"Daddy, I'm scared," Noah cried. "I saw monsters and they were..."

"Noah," Eric interrupted with irritation in his voice. "There's no such thing as monsters. Go back to sleep."

"I can't. I want to sleep with you," Noah sobbed.

Eric grabbed a teddy bear from a shelf and handed it to Noah. "Take your teddy and go back to sleep. Daddy has to get up early for work."

Eric tried to smile as his son continued crying: "Come on. You're a big boy. Go to sleep and Mommy will be here to wake you up in the morning."

Eric closed the door and returned to bed. Noah continued crying. Eric had heard somewhere that, if he ignored the crying, his child would soon give up and go to sleep. Instead, Noah cried louder and began to scream. Eric jumped out of bed a second time and stormed down the hallway. When he opened the door, Noah was sitting up, crying harder than before.

"What is wrong with you?" he demanded angrily. "I have to work tomorrow and you have preschool."

"The monsters came back," Noah sobbed. "I don't want to sleep by myself. I want Mommy!"

Eric grew more irritated. "I told you there's no such thing as monsters. Now stop crying and go to sleep!"

"I'm scared. Can you sleep in my bed, Daddy?"

Eric let out a loud sigh and checked his watch. How did it get to be so late?

"Okay, scoot over, sport. But you have to go to sleep," Eric pleaded.

After a few minutes, Noah quieted down and Eric crept off the bed. He closed the door and was halfway down the hall when Noah began crying again.

"Daddy! Daddy!"

Eric closed his bedroom door, crawled under the covers, and tried to ignore him. Noah continued begging Daddy to come back. Determined to teach his son to sleep on his own, Eric let him cry for nearly an hour before he gave in. He stomped to Noah's room, picked him up, and carried him back to the master bedroom. "Please, Noah, go to sleep now."

"Can you read me another story?"

Exasperated, Eric replied: "Noah, I swear. It's late. If you can't be quiet, I'm taking you back to your own room!"

Noah began crying again. They say to be consistent, Eric thought, so by God I'm going to be consistent. "I told you if you weren't quiet, I would take you back to your room." Eric scooped up his sobbing child from bed and carried him back to his own room. Noah screamed and cried as Eric tried in vain to return to sleep. Finally, he cried himself to sleep. The night was a disaster and both father and son were exhausted all the next day.

• • •

Like all parents, Eric made some mistakes. He was tired, impatient, and unsure of himself. Uncertainty and errors are part of the normal process of parenting. One thing we can do, however, is to learn from our mistakes. That's when problem-solving with another adult comes in handy. When you don't know what to do, sit down with your partner or, if you are single, talk with a friend, family member, or confidant, and figure out what to do next time. Eric and Rachel did just that. Eric did not want another sleepless night, and he did not want to feel like a rotten parent. Rachel wanted him to be more empathetic with their little boy (and Eric wanted that too). They set a few goals following strategies for good goal statements—make them clear, future oriented, positively framed, and specific:

- ☑ Rachel would visit Noah's preschool, talk with the staff, and spend time observing Noah and the other children. She wanted to know how they were caring for him, who the other kids were, and what the daily routines were. After all, monsters started appearing in the bedroom shortly after he started preschool.

☑ Eric would practice his active listening skills. He was pretty good at listening to others at work, with friends, and with his wife. He hadn't thought of applying those same skills with his son.

☑ Eric and Rachel would develop an incentive chart for Noah's bedtime routine that would include staying in his own bed at night.

Let's see how Eric applies the active listening technique with Noah the next night.

Eric tucks Noah in for the night. When he hears Noah begin to cry, he tells himself, "I'm going to be an understanding dad." He opens the door and asks gently, "Noah, what's wrong?"

"Daddy, I'm scared," Noah cries. "I saw monsters and they were moving by the window."

Eric turns on the light, sits on the bed beside his son, and strokes his hair. "You saw monsters by the window? You mean that window?" Eric says pointing.

"Yeah, that one," Noah says. Eric sees that the window is open, allowing a light breeze to billow the curtains. Eric smiles at his son as he stands up, and puffs out his chest to look strong. "There better not be anything there trying to scare my boy." Eric walks to the window and looks around outside. Then he shows Noah how the breeze coming in the open window causes the curtains to move and cast shadows on the wall. Eric closes and locks the window and pulls the curtains together.

"Alright, Noah. It was just the curtains blowing in the wind. With the streetlight shining through, I bet it looked like something was moving. But now the window is closed and locked and no monster can get in here." Eric turns off the bedroom light and sits down on the bed next to Noah. "Do you see anything moving, now?"

"No, but what if they come back?" Noah asks nervously.

Eric takes a deep breath. "Should we check the room?"

"Oh please."

"Just a second, buddy." Eric retrieves a flashlight from the hall closet.

"Can I look with you?" Noah asks.

"Sure. I could use your help to keep me brave, but then we have to go right back to bed."

Noah climbs down from the bed and joins his dad on the monster hunt. They look under the bed. "Clear," Eric says. "Let's check the closet." They approach the closet. Eric opens the door and shines the light from floor to ceiling. He pushes back the clothes hanging in the closet. "The closet is clear. Check?"

"Check," Noah says.

Eric notices that Noah has relaxed and is smiling: "I can see how this might be scary, but you are a brave boy. If there're any monsters, they are probably more scared of you. Let me hear you give a big roar.

"Arrrrh!" Noah growls.

Eric laughs and jumps as if startled: "Okay, Noah. Is there any other place to check?"

"Can you look under the bed one more time," Noah asks.

"You bet. Here, kneel down and look with me." There was nothing under the bed except a stray sock and a little dust. Eric picks up Noah's teddy bear, waves his hand over it, and says, "I hereby empower you to fight off all monsters and dragons. Your mission is to protect Noah." He hands Teddy to Noah and says: "I've given Teddy special magical powers. You hug him tight and any monsters that come into this room will be scared away. Ready for lights out?"

Noah hugs Teddy tightly, smiles at his superhero dad, and nods.

"Good. Now, let's get back in bed and off to sleep."

• • •

Eric and Rachel may have more work to do to settle Noah down at night and help him feel secure, but now they are on the right track. It takes practice to help kids enjoy the sanctity of their bedrooms. Tonight, Eric and Noah will both sleep better, and Eric does not feel like a monster dad. It took him only a few minutes to attend to Noah's fears. Instead of trying to talk some sense into a four-year-old mind, he explored the monster issue with him. He even found it rather enjoyable.

Did he reinforce Noah for staying up a little later and getting extra attention? Maybe so—for tonight. These parents may have more work to do to teach Noah to go to sleep on his own. But Eric listened to Noah's tale of woe without getting tied up with emotions—Noah's or his own. In this case, he only needed to acknowledge that something had frightened Noah and then take action to help ease that fear. He asked questions to better understand his child's perspective and showed respect by checking out areas where monsters might be lying in wait. Rachel will evaluate the preschool setting for issues that may be making Noah feel insecure. Transitions can create insecurities at first. Those are special occasions for parents to spend time actively listening to their children's fears and anxieties.

# Gaming the System

Parents in divorced families have to communicate with each other to establish house rules. They also have to listen to their children's point of view about living with the differences in rules in each parent's home. Here is an example.

Sal and Maria have a shared custody agreement for their ten-year-old son, Nico. Since their divorce a year ago, Sal and Maria have found themselves at odds at least a dozen times over their differing house rules. They rarely agree on anything. Maria is vegetarian and loathes television and video games. Sal's motto is anything in moderation. A burger or steak once or twice a week is fine. He allows Nico to watch TV shows about sports, science and history, and certain kids' shows. Sal believes video games—chosen wisely—help children develop cognitive abilities, especially logical, executive, and social skills.

Sal finally convinced Maria to allow Nico to play video games when he was at her house on alternate weeks, but only after Sal showed her reports confirming the games' positive benefits. Now they find themselves arguing over how much screen time Nico can have. Maria allows Nico to play each day after school for forty-five minutes. Sal lets his son play for up to two hours, as long as he has completed his homework and spent time outside playing with friends.

Nico knows the rules at each house. He thinks his mom is too strict and takes every opportunity to extend his screen time. One of the popular features of his favorite game is that it can be played on any computer, including tablets. Lately, Nico has been staying up past his 8:30 bedtime at mom's house and using his iPad beneath his blanket. Maria suspects he is breaking the rules. One night, she conducts a surprise inspection and catches Nico playing the game at 9 o'clock. She throws back the blanket and grabs the tablet.

"That's the last straw, young man. How many times have I told you that you get forty-five minutes and no playing after lights out," Maria yelled.

Nico nearly jumped out of his skin when Maria yanked back the covers. "Mom! Please, stop! You'll kill me and I'll have to start all over!"

"I don't care," Maria shouted. "You broke our rules!"

"Mom, I can explain," Nico pleaded. "I almost finished putting a wall around my city. I didn't mean to break the rules."

"You broke two rules. You went past forty-five minutes and you stayed up past your bedtime," Maria stated. "Actually you broke three rules. Sneaking around like this is the same as lying."

"Please, Mom. Let me show you."

"When I was your age we didn't play video games in bed, we read books." Maria stopped herself before going on a rant. She took several deep breaths. She did not want to have a major conflict when it was already past bedtime. She wanted to stay calm and let him know there would be consequences for his behavior. "Tomorrow, I'll tell you what chores you'll have for breaking the rules. Now, go to sleep. Tomorrow is a school day."

Dealing with disciplinary confrontations calls for regulating your emotions. Mom is furious at Nico. When she allowed time for video games, she was concerned he would become addicted and cheat on his time limit. She thinks her fears have come true.

Maria barely slept that night. As the hours wore on, she felt increasingly confused and guilty. She wasn't sure what to do about video games, but she did know what to do about the rule violations. The next morning, she got up earlier than usual and made a breakfast of smoothies from fresh organic fruit. She poured cereal into a bowl and waited for Nico to come down for breakfast. She had read some articles about his favorite game online earlier that morning and was surprised to see how some psychologists and teachers believe it is a good teaching tool.

Nico sat down at the table looking sullen. Maria handed him a glass with the smoothie. "Here you go," she said, trying to be cheerful. Nico took a few sips and stared at the kitchen table.

"Son, last night I wanted to take away your computer and video-game privileges forever. I am willing to discuss this with you, but not until you have had some consequences. You violated three rules and you will have to do three chores: clean the toilet bowl for sneaking, vacuum the living room and family room for the extra time you played, and sort the recycling box for staying up past your bedtime. I'm keeping your tablet until you've completed your chores. You can get started on the chores when you get home from school. When you're done, let's sit down and talk again. Tell me why I should allow you to play your game. I promise to listen."

Nico eyed her and sat up a little straighter. "I apologize. I shouldn't have stayed up and I shouldn't break your rules. But can I explain something?"

"Sure," she said. "We'll talk about it tonight after you're done your chores."

. . .

The Internet provides useful information about current technologies, games, and fads. Children today tend to stay on the cutting edge of these innovations, and parents need to know what they are doing. Although Nico's father had supplied convincing arguments in support of Nico's game, Maria wanted to equip herself with information, so she went to the Internet. But before talking with her son about it, she had to address the discipline situation. She started the morning pleasantly, admitted she had been angry, and calmly told her son what his consequences would be. When he asked to explain, she delayed the conversation until he had completed his chores. Maria was determined to practice her best listening skills with Nico later that day. Here's how the conversation unfolded.

"This game isn't like other games," Nico explained. "It teaches you cool stuff about how to save resources and how to work with other players to make cities and to make sure there's enough food for all the people. And you learn how to build things." Nico paused to see if his mom was listening. She looked directly at him and asked. "Could you show me how it works?"

"Oh, wow! Sure!" They got up and walked over to the computer. Nico asked, "Does this count against my screen time?"

Smiling, Maria said: "Of course not. You are teaching me. It seems pretty complicated. How did you learn how to do this?"

"Oh, my friend Will has been playing with his older brother. They have books, and Will even went to a coding workshop to get really good at it. He's been teaching me."

"You're learning how to write computer code?" Maria exclaimed. "Isn't that a pretty advanced skill? That's what programmers do. Show me how you build something."

Nico could barely contain himself as he set up the game. He showed her the wall he had been building around his city the previous night, explaining how he was creating it. She watched for a while and asked:, "How do you play with your friend when he's across town?"

"Well, it took us a while to get it synchronized, but now we have it down. You know, Mom," he continued, "a person really needs like a whole hour or two hours to accomplish anything. With forty-five minutes, you're just getting warmed up."

Maria nodded again and thought about what her son had just said. "I think I understand. Because you play this game with others, you need more time to play. I read up on this game today," she said. "It is pretty cool. I can see why kids like it, and I see what you mean about forty-five minutes being too short."

The boy's eyes lit up with anticipation. Maria continued: "I'm going to give you more time to play. How about an hour?"

Nico considered her offer. "Well, could we make it two hours like at Dad's?"

"Personally, I think that's too long for any screen time except a movie now and then," Maria replied. "I'll let you play for one hour."

"Can I have more time if I do an extra chore?" Nico was learning to negotiate with his mother without being demanding.

"Okay. That's fair," she said, "but here's the deal. You have to finish your homework first. And, you can earn up to one hour and thirty minutes total time per day. That means an extra fifteen minutes of game time for each extra fifteen-minute chore, with up to thirty minutes total. That's my final offer. Do you accept?"

"Yes. Deal!"

"Great. I'll write out an agreement and we'll both sign it," Maria said. "And here's your tablet back."

. . .

It's important to confine discipline to its own realm, separate from the relationship-building that grows from good communication. In the scenario above, Nico completed his disciplinary chores and paid for his rule violations. Now Mom and son are ready to negotiate a new agreement for video-game rules. Maria showed genuine interest in her son when she asked him to introduce her to the game. Until then, she had assumed it was just a waste of time and might become addictive. Although she would prefer that he spend time reading books, playing sports, or learning a musical instrument, she recognizes that today's kids love everything "tech." Setting aside her prejudices, Maria learned about her son's preoccupation. What better way to show interest in Nico than to ask him to teach her about the game he loves?

By communicating effectively with Nico, Maria discovered the game's complexity. She was surprised to find it interesting. A video game! She was impressed with his skill and the fact he knows how to play the game with friends across town. That also gave her a bit of a worry, however—she'd have to make sure she knew the kids he was playing with. She liked Nico's friend Will, but his brother was thirteen and she wondered what kind of influence he might be on a ten-year-old.

When Nico made his pitch for more time on the game, she listened and paraphrased his need for extended time. Imagine how Nico must have felt to know that his mom cared enough to read up on the game, and furthermore that she understood more time was needed to play it. The negotiation began when Nico asked for the same time that he was given at his dad's house—two hours. The negotiations proceeded with both sides gaining points. He could have up to ninety minutes a day (after homework) by putting in extra work at home. Both sides won a little and both sides gave a little. Notice that the steps were invariably small. These kinds of conversations build that spirit of cooperation we all seek in our family relationships. Use the active listening strategies to help you become a master listener, regardless of your child's age.

# Recap

Communication is a dance in which partners take turns leading and following (speaking and listening). Start out by choosing a good time and place for your conversations. It is seldom a good idea to talk when people are rushed, upset, or hungry. On the other hand, sometimes children need attention right away, as Troy did. Then it's important to make their concerns your priority. Review the indicators of emotions for clues about how your children may be feeling.

Some conversations flow more comfortably when you avoid eye contact. For these situations, consider taking a walk or talking in the car. Long drives provide the right atmosphere for meaningful discussions. We solved lots of family problems on the long drives to and from our weekend ski trips. The arsenic hour, just before meals when peoples' blood sugars are low, isn't a good time to talk either. On the other hand, bedtime can be an ideal time to settle down, review the day, and think about tomorrow. Every family has different schedules and rhythms, so identify the times that work and that don't work in yours. And then make sure that you actively listen to your children when they need your attention.

## Practice Assignment

Do one of these two activities to enhance your active listening skills.

### Collages

A collage is an artistic work made by pasting materials, pictures, and sometimes objects onto a surface. You can even write or draw on it. The activity is especially effective with younger children. Parents use magazines, comic books, catalogs, and other sources for images and text. According to parents and kids, collages are one of their favorite practice activities.

- ☑ Set aside a special time. Tell your children you're going to make a collage that tells stories about children, activities, families, and feelings. While you work together on the collage, encourage them to make up stories about the people and situations in the collage. Ask questions that lead to storytelling about the people—what they're doing, how they feel. Practice active listening strategies while you do this exercise.

- ☑ The purpose of the activity is to encourage conversation with your children with a focus on your listening. There is no right or wrong way to do this. Just give your children an opportunity to talk about feelings, thoughts, events. It is often easier for them to talk about people in the picture than about themselves.

## Daily Debriefings

Each day, debrief with your children. Establish a five- to ten-minute period to talk about the people and events in their lives. Be sensitive to the way they feel about these things. Ask one or two questions about specific activities that took place. For instance: "Tell me about one thing that happened while you were at Khalea's house." For some children, it's helpful to ask a global question like: "What is one fun thing you did today?" During the school year, the questions may focus on school activities: "What did you work on in reading today?" or "What is the topic in science right now?" Use active listening strategies and practice one or two specific listening behaviors that are hard for you.

# Chapter Seven

# We Can Work It Out

---

Families need to solve problems every day. Some are common and straightforward: How do we get the kids from here to there? What will we fix for dinner? Others are more complicated: How do we deal with mounting conflicts among the kids? Who will pick up the kids when we both have to work late. Some problems are unique to your own family structure. Single parents, newly divorcing parents, and parents in step- or blended families may have to deal with different kinds of issues. Some problems may not even have solutions—or at least not solutions that are satisfying. The way we perceive and address problems depends on our individual personalities, our children's personalities, stress levels, and available resources. Issues that are simple for you to resolve may seem impossible to me.

Although the potential for problems is almost limitless, we have found that holding family meetings is a highly effective technique for resolving them. Family meetings build on most of the skills you have learned so far—especially goal setting, teaching through encouragement, regulating emotions, and active listening. Regardless of the problem and family structure in your household, a family meeting is an effective way to engage your children in the problem-solving process and to teach them to cooperate, collaborate, and contribute.

# The Best-Laid Plans. . .

Let's take a look at how one family uses effective problem-solving techniques in a family meeting.

Remember Daniella and Cesar, who were dealing with conflicts surrounding the morning bathroom routine? They found the problem was creeping into their conversations, until they realized something had to be done.

Cesar began the conversation with a reality check. "We can't add a new bathroom," he said, "so they'll just have to deal with it. And they're not using ours. Neither one of us would get to work on time."

Daniella agreed: "Clearly the kids can't work this out by themselves, so we'd better do something now or we'll all go crazy." Daniella, who had become a fan of goal-setting, pulled out a notepad and pen from the nightstand. Cesar smiled as he watched his wife move into action.

"So what do we want to happen?" she asked. Without pausing for Cesar's response, she went on: "We want Ava to get ready for school and out the door pleasantly, right? The problem is the bathroom, so what steps can we take to get her out of there and leave the boys enough time to do their thing?"

"Do you know what she is doing every morning that takes nearly an hour?" Cesar asked.

"Fixing her hair and primping in front of the mirror," Daniella answered.

"Does she have to do it in the bathroom?"

Daniella laughed: "That's where the mirror is so that's where our daughter is."

Daniella and Cesar looked at each other and came to the same realization. Cesar said, "We have to get her a mirror."

"With a vanity," Daniella added.

Before sending the children off to school, Cesar announced: "Kids, we're having a family meeting after dinner tonight to solve this bathroom problem."

"Finally," Benito said, glaring at his sister.

• • •

Families often get stuck *worrying* about their problems rather than figuring out how to resolve them. Daniella and Cesar had been living too long with chaos and conflict on school mornings. Every family member was caught in the uproar: child versus child, parent versus child, and sometimes parent versus parent. They were beginning to think the problem would never be resolved. To get some peace, the family needed a problem-solving strategy. The first step, which Daniella has already taken, is to define what they want with a goal statement.

Goal statements address what you *can* do. During the couple's initial discussion, Cesar made several "can't" statements: We can't add a new bathroom. The kids can't work it out. They can't use our bathroom. Fortunately, Cesar and Daniella work as a team, so at least one person can focus on a solution, even if the other despairs of change.

Wisely, Daniella let Cesar's "can't" statements pass and instead asked: What do we want? This question serves as a prompt for positive statements that promote positive thinking. When you shift attention toward a goal, you turn away from the past (or unpleasant present) and focus on fixing the problem.

Cesar's question about what took Ava so long led the couple to a mutual "Aha!" moment. She needs a mirror! Now the issue is about mirrors, rather than the things Cesar says can't be done. Together, he and Daniella make a plan.

With a plan in hand, Cesar announced a family meeting to discuss the bathroom issue. This couple's united parenting front—a skill we will describe in chapter 10—is a blessing not all families enjoy. If you have this luxury already, you are indeed lucky. For now, notice that this couple designed and agreed on a plan *before* discussing it with the kids. Watch how they engage the children in brainstorming ideas as a family.

That evening, the kids took their seats on the couch and Daniella started the meeting.

"We have two bathrooms and five people in this house. When you were little, everything worked fine. But now that Ava is getting older, she needs more time to get ready in the morning. The fighting is always about the bathroom. So how can everyone cooperate and share the bathroom so we can have peace in the mornings?"

Benito blurted out: "She was in there for one hour and six minutes this morning."

"Are you're timing me, you little. . .?"

Cesar quickly intervened: "Ava! Benito! We're having a meeting. Everybody gets a turn. You're all getting older and we need to work out a new routine for the bathroom. Boys, do you have any helpful suggestions on what we can do?"

"Make her get up earlier if she wants to stay in the bathroom so long," Benito said.

Ava frowned, as Daniella wrote down Benito's suggestion on the small whiteboard she used for brainstorming sessions. "Okay. That's one possibility. Miguel?"

"Yeah, make her get up early."

"Okay." Daniella made a check mark next to Benito's suggestion.

"Ava?"

"Get a litter box for their room," Ava snarled.

Cesar jumped in: "Ava, we're trying to help you, so be nice, please. Now, what's taking up most of your time?"

Ava pulled her hair out of a ponytail, curls springing into action. "Maybe this? Thanks for the genes, Dad."

Cesar also had a full head of thick curly hair. "The family curse," he joked.

"Boys, you take baths before bed, so you just need the bathroom in the mornings to wash your faces and brush your teeth," Daniella said. "Anything else besides the obvious?" The boys shook their heads.

Cesar stood up. "Here's what your mom and I think. Ava, if we get you a vanity with a mirror for your bedroom, can you shower and be out of the bathroom by 6:00?"

"OMG! Are you serious? Yes. Yes, yes, yes!"

"Boys, if your sister is out of the bathroom by 6:00, will you have enough bathroom time?"

"Yeah, but what if she doesn't get out by 6:00?" Benito replied.

"Hmm. Good point." Daniella turned to Ava and asked: "What about that?"

"I promise to be out by 6:00. I don't need more time if I have my own vanity and mirror."

"Okay. Ava, you can have the bathroom until 6:00, and then you agree to give it up to the boys. And boys, don't hassle your sister before 6:00. If all agree, our meeting is adjourned."

· · ·

This is teamwork in action. As Daniella led the family meeting, Cesar refereed, managing the children's zings and zaps. Daniella set the stage for family problem-solving by stating the issue—the fighting is about the bathroom; Ava needs more time to fix her hair. Then she prompted a goal statement with the question: How can the kids peacefully share the bathroom?

When Benito and Ava jumped into blame mode, Cesar took several proactive steps. He interrupted them, reminded them that everyone would have a turn, stated the goal of working out a new routine, and started the brainstorming process by asking the boys for suggestions. Daniella wrote down suggestions, and did not react to negatively tinged ideas. Cesar directed traffic when the boys attacked and moved the brainstorming forward by prompting Ava with a question. He joined Ava with a humorous response about the hair gene.

Notice that the parents asked their children for ideas *before* introducing their own suggestion. The idea to get Ava a vanity led the discussion to a quick resolution. Daniella restated the plan—Ava has the bathroom until 6:00; the boys don't hassle her until then. Ava gets a vanity. Of course, Cesar and Daniella could have bought a cheap vanity and mirror without a family discussion. But can you see the benefits the parents and children gained by solving the problem together?

Learning to cooperate as a family doesn't happen on its own. Solving problems together through regular family meetings is a foundational parenting skill and you set an example for your children to follow at school and with their own families when they grow up. Here are our strategies for family problem-solving.

# Strategies for Problem-Solving

## Make a goal statement:

- Focus on the future.
- Be short and specific.
- Be positive.
- State what is desired.

## Brainstorm solutions:

- Engage the children.
- Be creative.
- Accept all ideas as good ideas.
- Be open.

## Consider solutions:

- Cross off ideas that won't work.
- Discuss pros and cons.
- Ask: Will it work?

## Make a plan:

- Combine solutions.
- Be realistic.

## Write an agreement:

- Be specific.

☐ Get signatures.

☐ Reward success.

## Try it out!

After the kids went to bed, Daniella and Cesar made a plan for purchasing a used vanity that Ava could refinish to her own taste. Then they considered ways to include the boys in the process. "While you're out with Ava," Cesar suggested, "I'll take them to the store that sells used video games. They can each pick one and we'll keep the cost for everything under a hundred dollars." You can see how Daniella and Cesar quickly designed the next step in their path toward morning peace. Motivated to prevent another school-morning conflict, they decided to take immediate action. Each parent contributed ideas for the plan, and they split the tasks between them. As they thought about their options, they combined ideas. They set a price limit for Ava and agreed to get something for the boys to be fair. They solved the problem as partners.

The next morning at breakfast, Cesar explained the plan to Ava and the boys. As expected, Ava insisted she needed a new vanity, but her parents stood firm. By midafternoon, she was in the garage painting her second-hand vanity. By Sunday afternoon, she had every drawer lined and filled and was sitting in front of the mirror brushing her hair.

Mornings were peaceful for the next three weeks. Then, all hell broke loose again. (It usually does, so be ready.) Cesar and Daniella were getting dressed when they heard Benito and Miguel banging on the bathroom door and yelling at Ava. Cesar shook his head and looked at Daniella for moral support: "Is this Groundhog Day? Do I look like Bill Murray?"

 Cesar marched down the hall. The boys stopped yelling the moment they saw Cesar's furrowed brow and blazing eyes.

"Dad, look," Benito said, pointing at the closed bathroom door and then to his watch. "It's 6:15 and she's still in there!" Miguel was squirming and holding the front of his pajama bottoms. "Daddy, I have to pee really bad."

"Go ahead and use my bathroom, Miguel." Cesar said, exasperated. "Ava! Wrap it up and give the bathroom to the boys."

"Ava's been taking longer and longer again, Dad," Benito complained, then yelled at the closed door. "Get out of there, you selfish b...b...witch!"

Cesar's eyes widened. He snapped his fingers and pointed at Benito. Ava opened the bathroom door, letting out a roiling cloud of steam. "Oh. So sorry, Benito. No hot water left, jerk!"

Daniella joined the melee: "What is going on here? I thought this was settled!"

"Ava, you are making us all late this morning. We will talk about this after dinner tonight. For now, let's get going."

• • •

When this family took the final step and tried out their plan, they learned what they had to do next—make a plan for those times when the agreement is violated. Nothing is ever as easy as it seems on paper, so parents always need a Plan B. Families often tell us that their first tries don't work perfectly. Of course they don't. Although they may start out well, we all encounter bumps in the road. In this case, peace slipped back into chaos when Ava broke her part of the bargain. When harsh words began to fly, it was time for everyone to disengage and meet later that day, after people calmed down. During the break, Daniella realized that, instead of abandoning their original plan, they simply needed to add to it.

Notice that the last steps of the problem-solving technique call for writing out an agreement and getting everyone to sign it. Daniella and Cesar forgot that step on the first round. So they had another meeting to spell out the details of the family agreement and had everyone certify their approval with signatures.

# Family Meetings

Family meetings work best when they incorporate problem-solving strategies and engage the children in planning, establishing rules and regulations, and resolving conflicts. When Daniella and Cesar started holding family meetings, their children were pleased to be involved in the process. Their participation increased their buy-in. Cesar and Daniella explained that meetings would take place at least once a week and last for about fifteen minutes. Each meeting would focus on a specific topic—like planning a fun family activity, addressing disagreements, making house rules, and establishing consequences for violating them. Family members would be expected to stay on topic during meetings. Extra meetings would be scheduled to address additional topics.

The children helped make up the list of ground rules: be polite, wait your turn, keep it short, stay calm, stay on topic, no phones/texting. Daniella and Cesar agreed to take turns serving as meeting chair or referee. The chair led the meetings using problem-solving strategies; the referee tracked rule violations and asked anyone with three violations to take a five-minute break from the meeting. In case of chaos, the referee stopped the meeting. To motivate the children to cooperate, the parents offered dessert as an incentive following a successful meeting. Success was defined as everyone participating without three rule violations during the meeting. Resolving the issue at hand during the meeting was not required to earn dessert. At each meeting, a different child was allowed to choose the dessert incentive.

Here are some strategies that can lead to harmonious and productive family meetings, and some suggestions for establishing ground rules for your own family meetings.

## Strategies for Family Meetings

- Plan ahead for no interruptions.
- Establish ground rules.
- Make good goal statements.
- Model active listening.
- Summarize what has been said.
- Enforce ground rules.
- Make sure everyone has a chance to talk.
- Model how to regulate emotions.
- Move the conversation forward.
- Keep the meeting short and interesting.
- Review agreements.
- Follow through with rewards for good meeting behavior.

## Ground Rules for Family Meetings

- Be polite.
- Wait your turn.
- Keep it short.
- Stay calm.
- Stay on topic.
- No phones/no texting.

Until everyone in the family gets the hang of it, review the rules and post a copy as a reminder.

Here's how Daniella and Cesar ran the family meeting that dealt with the Ava's failure to abide by the family agreement reached about bathroom use.

 Dinner was quiet. Daniella and Cesar exchanged surprised glances as the kids ate without arguing over the last of the mac and cheese. After the morning's meltdown, Benito and Ava were still tense. Once everyone was seated, Daniella opened the meeting. Cesar served as the referee to keep the meeting moving and on topic. Daniella glanced at her watch. "Okay. Let's keep this to fifteen minutes. The purpose of our meeting tonight is to address this morning's breakdown and come up with an appropriate solution. Let's start with Ava."

Daniella turned to face Ava, who was slumped on the couch. "Ava, we gave you a vanity so you would not have to spend so much time in the bathroom. In exchange, you agreed to be out of the bathroom by 6:00. You violated your agreement today."

"No," Ava whined. "I just needed more time."

"B.S.," Benito muttered.

Cesar put a check mark next to Benito's name on a notepad. "Keep it civil, Benito. That's one strike." Cesar and Daniella permitted two strikes, with a third rule violation earning a five-minute break from the meeting. Miguel sat quietly next to his brother, reminding himself to keep out of the fray. No violations earned points that could be redeemed later for cash, treats, or extra privileges. Miguel intended to make the meeting profitable.

"It's time to set some consequences for violating the rules," Daniella continued. "Ava was late leaving the bathroom and the boys broke the peace by shouting and pounding on the door."

Ava started to speak, then hesitated. "This is so stupid," she said, glancing at her brothers and her dad, who was making a check mark next to her name. "Aw, Dad, come on!"

Cesar put another check next to her name and held up two fingers. Ava crossed her arms and slumped farther into the couch.

"Ava, do we need to change your routine to help you share the bathroom with your brothers?" Daniella asked.

With dejection, Ava softly said "no" and stared at the floor.

Suddenly, Daniella's cell phone rang. Cesar smiled at his wife and put a check mark by her name. "The rules apply to everyone," Cesar stated. The boys laughed, while Ava remained sullen. Daniella turned off the ringer on her phone. "Oops. My bad," she chuckled, as she studied Ava's closed body language and stressed expression.

"Ava, do you have any ideas how to get back on our morning schedule?" Daniella asked.

"Not really," Ava replied politely.

Benito raised his hand. Daniella nodded to give him the floor.

"Maybe Ava needs to get up earlier," Benito suggested.

Cesar wrote down Benito's suggestion as Ava glared at her brother.

"Miguel, any ideas," Daniella asked.

"Maybe Ava could cut her hair so she doesn't have to mess with it so much," Miguel said.

"That is a dumb idea," Ava retorted, flaring her nostrils at Miguel.

"Hey, there are no dumb ideas when we're trying to brainstorm," Cesar said, writing down Miguel's suggestion.

"Ava, we could really use your input here," Daniella said. "What do you need to do to get out of the bathroom on schedule?"

"I'll just be faster, okay?" Ava said, looking sincerely dejected. "And, can you or Dad let me know when it's 6:00?"

Daniella looked at Cesar. "Okay. Ava, you'll try harder to be out of the bathroom by 6:00."

Cesar looked up as he wrote down Ava's suggestion, "So, that would mean Mom and I would set a timer for 6:00 and let Ava know when her time's up."

Daniella looked at Cesar's list. "Ava to get up earlier; Ava to cut her hair; Ava to be faster; Mom or Dad to be timekeepers. Any more ideas?"

Heads were shaking around the room.

"Does anyone want to eliminate any of these?"

"I don't like the idea of Ava cutting her hair—unless she wants to, that is," said Daniella.

Ava muttered, "I don't want to get up earlier. I'll try harder."

Cesar said: "I like the idea for Mom and me to be the timekeepers. That would keep Benito and Miguel from tattling, and maybe keep them from shouting and pounding on the door as well."

"Shall we go with two ideas combined: Ava to try harder and Mom or Dad to set a timer to let Ava know when it's 6:00?" Daniella asked.

When everyone nodded, Cesar said: "Okay, then. And, oh yes, there's a part two to this issue. Your mom and I discussed the need for a consequence when you break the rules. Ava, if you keep the boys waiting past 6:00 again, you will get an extra chore to do. And boys, shouting and banging on the door will get you an extra chore too. These rules go into effect immediately."

"Our last piece of business is the way all of you behaved this morning. For that, all three of you have an extra chore," Daniella said. "Ava will wash tonight's dishes and Miguel will dry them. Benito will sweep the patio and driveway. No tech or TV until your chores are done. We will have dessert after the chores are done."

Miguel lost his angelic composure and started to protest: "But I didn't do anything."

"All three of you were shouting and both of you boys pounded on the door," Daniella reminded them. "We won't have that behavior again."

"Everybody got it?" Cesar asked. The children nodded agreement. "Okay, I'm going to write up this agreement and I'll collect your signatures over dessert. Meeting adjourned. Do your chores now so we can have dessert. Ava, what dessert do you want to pick?"

"I'll let Miguel have my turn," she said.

• • •

It would be easy to miss the strategies that Daniella and Cesar used to run this family meeting, because they worked so well. Notice how they applied the problem-solving strategies suggested above.

☑ The meeting was scheduled for a specific time (after dinner).

☑ Cesar reviewed the family meeting format and provided a printed list of ground rules.

☑ Goal statements were made: The purpose was to address the meltdown, find an appropriate solution, and set consequences. These goals directed the meeting.

☑ The parents engaged all the children in the brainstorming process. When Ava criticized Miguel's suggestion, she was reminded that all ideas are included while brainstorming.

☑ Cesar calmly enforced ground rules with a check mark and held up one or two fingers to silently punctuate violations. Notice that the parents were also subject to the rules.

☑ Daniella signaled the end of the brainstorming process by summarizing the ideas.

☑ Some ideas were easily eliminated, and two ideas were endorsed.

☑ Once an agreement was reached, the parents moved on to set consequences for the morning's chaos.

☑ The disciplinary chores were to be completed after the meeting and before dessert. Ava was paired with Miguel to do the dishes and Benito was given a job on his own, which would keep him from arguing with his sibs.

☑ Cesar wrote up the agreement, and a new plan to promote morning peace was in place.

Their next step was to try it out and hope this version would last longer than three weeks.

# Recap

Different family circumstances call for different approaches to family problem-solving. If you have young children, consider using tokens to engage them appropriately. For example, structure the session, labeling each step along the way: Okay, our goal is to figure out something fun we can do this weekend. What are some ideas? Remember, the sky is the limit while brainstorming. To help children cooperate, use your favorite form of tokens for following procedures and offer a small reward for earning a set number of tokens. Ask prompting questions to help children participate successfully. For example, once you have made up a list of ideas to address the issue, ask a prompting question: Are there any ideas we should cross out? Modeling appropriate behavior is particularly important with little ones. And be sure to start with fun issues that will be easy to resolve.

If you are parenting alone, it helps to prepare. Some parents consult friends or family members and have some ideas in mind before they engage their children. Write down your goal so that, if you get sidetracked, you have a cheat sheet to redirect the meeting. Some single parents find it easiest to practice problem-solving with one child at a time before managing the whole family. In a later chapter, we offer strategies for managing conflict during family meetings that address touchy topics.

## *Practice Assignment*

Call a family meeting and introduce the meeting strategies. Use the first meeting to plan a fun family event. Make the event something that is easy to do. It doesn't have to be a trip to the zoo, or to go on a camping trip. It can be something as small as playing a game together in the evening or planning a picnic dinner in the yard. First, establish ground rules for the meeting using the problem-solving worksheet below as a guide. Write out your agreement, including all important details: who, when, where, what, and how. Then carry out the fun family event.

## Problem–Solving Worksheet

**Step 1. Make a good goal statement.**

**Step 2. Brainstorm solutions.**

**Step 3. Consider solutions:**

☑ Can we agree to cross any solutions off the list?

☑ What are the advantages and disadvantages of each solution?

**Step 4. Combine, choose, make a plan:**

☑ Combine ideas, consider other solutions, choose.

☑ Be realistic as you create your plan.

**Step 5. Write an agreement.**

☑ Include who will do what by when and the incentive.

☑ Date it and have everyone sign it

**Step 6: Try it out.**

# Chapter Eight

# Someone to Watch Over Me

P rotecting children from harm is one of the strongest parenting instincts. In nature, this instinct is pretty straightforward—a bear simply attacks anything that threatens its offspring. For us, on the other hand, monitoring and protecting our children has become one of the most complex parenting skills we must develop. From infancy through the late teen years (nearly two decades), we have to ensure that our children are safe and engaged in desirable activities with desirable peers. We have to worry about bad influences, car pools, teacher-parent conferences, exposure to raunchy television shows and Internet sites, and potential weirdos in the community. And, to make it even more difficult, the demands of our children and the hazards of our society keep changing as our children mature.

Think about the ways you kept track of your children's whereabouts and activities when they were toddlers roaming throughout the house, then when they started to play outside, then when they started preschool and then first grade. Then, they started going out with peers on their own and—heaven help us—they started to drive or ride with kids who drive. Parents with more than one child know that the level of monitoring required also depends on each child's temperament, their individual levels of functioning, and their widely varying personal interests. Some kids are always on the move, pushing the limits; others avoid exploration. A parent's challenges also differ for each child.

Regardless of your children's ages, you need to know where they are, what they're doing, who they're with, the safety of the environment, and how they get to and from their activities. Of course, you can use technology to plant cameras around the house, or sew tracking devices into their clothes. But in this chapter, we won't talk about becoming some sort of Orwellian Big Brother. Instead, we'll talk about applying common sense in everyday situations to monitor our children and keep them safe.

With toddlers, you need to know where they are in the house and the potential dangers in each room. A toddler left alone for two minutes is an accident waiting to happen. When children are outside, you need to keep an eye on the neighborhood, the neighbors, and the people who visit the neighbors. When you leave children in other people's care, you have to consider the quality of the caregivers and the environments they provide. And then there is school. Do you know their teachers? Do your children follow rules? How well do they get along with others? How often do you check?

We all want our children to explore and discover the magic in their environments. But while children need freedom and independence, we also want to ensure they are safe. As their independence grows, we adjust the strategies we use and determine how much we monitor their activities.

Overall, the amount of freedom you give your children is based on *their* responsible and competent behavior. Do they go where they say they are going? Some parents make quick random drop-ins to check up. When your children come home from an event, how do they appear? Are they upset? Have stories to tell? Are they disheveled? Wearing clothes they didn't have on when they left? Wearing makeup? Smelling of smoke or alcohol? Do they tell the truth? Children who lie warrant closer monitoring. Although they will accuse you of not trusting them, trust must be earned, especially for those who don't always tell the truth. Do they come home on time? Hang out with good kids? If their friends seem disreputable or often get in trouble, keep a closer watch on your child. Good kids can be led astray when they have unsupervised time with peers who get in trouble. If you establish solid monitoring routines when your children are young, they will better accept continued monitoring as they grow older,

Many parents find it handy to follow a checklist when their children are going out. Some parents post the list on their back door or program it into their smartphones. Here are the key questions to ask:

☑ *Where* are you going?

☑ *Who* will be there?

☑ *What* will you be doing?

☑ *When* will you be home?

☑ *How* will you get there and back?

## Social Media

In today's society, parents must contend with their children's use of social media. In the recent past, we only had to worry about watching appropriate TV shows or who they were talking to on the telephone. Now we have to monitor how and with whom our children are engaging on Twitter, Instagram, Snapchat, Facebook, and other emerging programs. Monitoring social media may seem overwhelming if you don't already use it, but it is especially helpful when you have to be away from home. It's easy to learn. Ask a tech-savvy parent, relative, or your child's teacher. You will be surprised at what you can discover about your children, their friends (and, yes, their teachers, too) with the right keystrokes. Here's an example of how one set of parents handled the challenge.

 After months of discussion, Jennifer and her husband, David, decided to allow their twelve-year-old son to set up Facebook and Twitter accounts. The condition was that Patrick had to include Mom and Dad among his "friends" and "followers."

David had mixed feelings about how old children should be to use social media, but he became a supporter one Saturday morning when he had to work at the office while Jennifer was out of town.

"Before I drove to my office," David told Jennifer, "Patrick asked if he could meet some friends at a park a few blocks from our house to toss a football around. We have a close-knit neighborhood where everybody knows each other, so I said fine."

David had set his smartphone to receive an alert whenever Patrick posted an update on Facebook or sent a tweet. He was at his desk less than fifteen minutes when his phone pinged. Patrick posted this update on his status: "All comers. Let's get dirty. No pads. Park in 30."

David and Jennifer allowed Patrick to play football on a team with a coach, but a pickup game of tackle without pads? No way. He was about to call Patrick and put the kibosh on this when his phone started pinging again. One of the kids messaged: "Will there be any grown-ups?" Patrick responded: "No." The other child responded that he couldn't come. One by one, the other boys dropped out as well. "Until then," David said, "I hadn't realized what a handy tool social media can be for monitoring Patrick's behavior—and that of his friends and their parents."

David noted which boy had asked if parents were attending, found his mom on Facebook, and sent her a message thanking her for paying attention. "I kind of feel like I'm spying, but I was impressed by the ability to see what Patrick was doing in real time without following him around," he said.

• • •

Children frequently test their parents' boundaries. It's in their DNA. If nobody is watching, why not break the rules—after all, what are the consequences? Patrick's parents have clearly established rules—they allow football on a team with proper equipment and a coach; tackle football without adult supervision is off limits. David had no problem allowing Patrick to hang out in the park with his friends, because he knew the neighborhood was safe. Had they lived in a dangerous neighborhood, unsupervised street time might require more monitoring.

David was on top of his parenting game in the way he used social media. Not only did he keep track of his son's posts, he also connected positively with a parent in his son's social network. What better way to know what goes on between your children and their peers than to tune in on their posts and tweets! Contacting the friend's mother established a line of communication with a like-minded parent.

Of course, once David caught Patrick breaking the rules, he had to follow up with a negative consequence. It was fall and there were leaves to rake. When kids know they will pay for breaking rules, they usually think twice. In Patrick's case, in addition to his disciplinary chore, his parents may want to increase their watchfulness until he earns back their trust.

Monitoring is simplified when you engage children in supervised activities that are fun and age-appropriate, and that provide learning opportunities. What kinds of resources are available in your neighborhood? Are trustworthy adults present who can keep an eye out and promote safety? In Patrick's case, if he had been able to get a group of boys to play tackle football without supervision, someone could have ended up with a concussion or a broken bone, and perhaps even a lawsuit depending on the density of attorneys in your neighborhood.

## Childcare and Babysitters

Working parents require reliable childcare. Families base their arrangements on their financial resources, personal values, and the special needs and interests of their children. Some use daycare centers; some have private babysitters; others have full- or part-time nannies. Regardless, certain principles are the same whether you use a nanny or a daycare center. Most parents want their children to be in a safe environment with attentive and nurturing caregivers who engage children in skill-building activities that are appropriate for each child's developmental phase, capabilities, and interests. How can you be confident that you have chosen a good provider and a safe setting for your child?

You can start by vetting the provider and caregiving environment. Check the Internet for reviews and checklists. Make a site visit. Make your own checklist and discuss whatever is important to you. Once you have chosen a childcare provider, spend a few minutes to watch how the staff members interact with other children and parents.

The transition to preschool can be especially difficult for some children and some parents. During the first weeks, parents must determine if new problems are emerging from the change itself, the preschool, a particular person or situation at the school, or a random circumstance unrelated to the transition. Transitions to new schools when you move or when children advance to middle school or high school are often challenging as well. When there are problems, ask your children about them. Unfortunately, most preschoolers don't have the words to explain why they feel unhappy or uneasy, and older children may be reluctant to share their problems. At best, you may have to glean hints from the way they act or comments they make. Regardless, remember to regulate your emotions—stay neutral. Of course, this is scary for you, but if you come across as overly concerned, you may unknowingly reinforce your children's desire to stay home with you.

Remember Noah, the four-year-old with monsters in his bedroom? Let's see how his parents worked on that problem.

 Rachel and Eric wondered why their son's nightmares had begun around the same time he started preschool. Maybe it had to do with being separated from his parents, or maybe something was occurring at school. They decided it would be a good idea for Rachel to observe at the preschool for an hour after dropping off Noah.

"You know the school doesn't like it when parents linger," Eric said.

"That's their problem. We're paying a fortune for him to be there, so I'm going to stick around and see if something is wrong," Rachel said.

Rachel woke Noah at 7:00 and encouraged him through his morning routine, checking off each step on his incentive chart: Wash hands and face. Get dressed. Eat breakfast. Brush teeth. Ready on time. He earned a treat for his lunchbox because he did so well. As Rachel buckled him into his car seat, she asked: "Are you excited to be going to school?"

Noah looked down and said: "I guess so."

"Is anything bothering you?"

"I want to stay home with you, Mommy."

"Oh, that would be nice," Rachel answered, "but Mommy needs to sleep so she can have lots of energy to play when you get home and make dinner for you and Daddy."

"I like Daddy's cooking better," Noah teased.

Rachel laughed. "Well, Daddy can make us dinner tomorrow." Rachel drove in silence to see if Noah would say anything else about preschool. After a few minutes, she returned to the subject: "I know school is new for you, but you'll be fine. Just listen to your teachers and be nice to the other kids."

. . .

Rachel has set Noah up well for his day at school. She's using an incentive chart to help him cooperate through the morning routine, and the question she asks about school is positively framed: Are you excited to be going to school? A less productive approach might be to ask if he were afraid of something at school, which would reinforce his reluctance to adapt to a new setting. When Noah indicated that he wanted to stay home, Rachel made light of it and turned the conversation to something slightly humorous.

 When they arrived at the preschool, Rachel walked Noah inside. As she signed him in, the head teacher said: "Good morning, Rachel. We'll take it from here."

"I'm going to stay on for a little while. I'll be a fly on the wall. You won't know I'm here," Rachel said politely.

"Oh. I'm sorry. You need to make an appointment for that. Otherwise, we would have as many parents here as children," the teacher said.

"I'll be sure to do that next time. But I'm staying for a little while now."

The teacher hesitated: "I'm afraid that's not how we do things."

"I'm sure you can make an exception. Today is my day off." Rachel had decided she would observe or she would take Noah home. Her facial expression told the teacher all she needed to know.

"You can sit in the back, but please don't interrupt the children or the teachers," she said. She turned and walked down the hall back to her office, heels clicking against the polished tile floor.

Rachel introduced herself to Noah's teacher and told her she would be observing for an hour. "Oh? Well, I suppose. . ." the teacher said. Rachel thanked her and quietly found her seat.

For the first ten minutes, Noah wandered between clusters of children. The kids seemed to ignore him. Dejected, he found a coloring book and crayons and sat down on the floor. Rachel's heart ached, but she reminded herself that Noah had only started school a couple of weeks earlier.

The teacher and an aide were preoccupied with a group of boys arguing over a set of action figures. Another aide was cleaning up a spill. As Noah colored, a girl approached and said something that upset him. Rachel had to use all of her self-control to keep from intervening. The girl, who was bigger than Noah, reached down and snatched a handful of crayons. Noah stood up and walked away to another corner of the room. As the girl took over the coloring book, Noah sat alone in the corner looking anxious.

The teachers broke up the squabble between the boys, but they missed the interaction between Noah and the girl. They gossiped among themselves as Noah finally found a picture book and began slowly turning the pages. Rachel scribbled notes on a small pad she kept in her purse. She was pleased that Noah handled the situation without a fuss, although she was angry that the bully's behavior went unnoticed. How many other times had this occurred? Rachel was not pleased, as she left quietly.

• • •

Rachel handled the interaction with the head teacher well. She started the conversation in a positive and matter-of-fact manner, indicating that she was planning to observe. When the teacher tried to prevent this, Rachel simply made it clear with words and nonverbal cues that she would not be deterred. While she watched, she noted that the teachers and aides paid more attention to children who made a scene than to a shy child who was new to the class. She noted that the school was clean and well-organized and provided engaging toys and activities. But she did not like the teacher's reluctance to let her observe. Fancy school or not, all parents have the right to know what's happening when their children are in the care of others.

The experience gnawed at Rachel for days. Eric had chosen the school because of its reputation as "the finest preschool" in the city. Eric had put Noah on the preschool's waiting list the day after he was born. Rachel knew what Eric would say if she wanted to move Noah to a different environment. He would argue that Noah's attendance there would guarantee his acceptance to the best private elementary and high schools and help him get into an Ivy League university. The fact that the preschool cost a small fortune, he felt, showed their dedication as parents. Rachel believed the money would be better spent on a family vacation and saving for that Ivy League school years ahead. However, she reminded herself to keep her biases out of her current concern.

Rachel made an appointment to talk with the head teacher about her observations and Noah's ongoing reluctance to attend school. The teacher tried to reassure her that timid children take longer to adjust and that Noah would be just fine with a little time. Rachel explained that the active kids seemed to get more attention, while quiet children like Noah were ignored. The teacher became defensive. When Rachel tried to talk with Noah later about the school, his response was to cry. "I just want to stay at home with you, Mommy," he blurted between sobs.

That evening after Noah went to bed, Rachel told Eric about her observations, her conversation with the teacher, and Noah's tearful wish to stay at home.

Eric argued exactly as predicted. When he was finished, Rachel said: "Our little boy is miserable at that preschool."

"I'm trying to give him the best future possible," Eric countered.

"I understand that, but I want to give him the best *today* possible," Rachel replied.

Eric considered her words. If he insisted on staying with the school, Noah might adjust and come to love it, and then Rachel would be happy too. One day they would both thank him. But if Noah continued to be unhappy, life would become miserable. He felt he was right in wanting the best school for Noah. But maybe in this case the "best" school was not the right school for their son. "Let's have a family meeting, tomorrow," Eric conceded.

At the meeting, Eric and Rachel both helped Noah explain how he felt about the school. Checking their emotions and being careful not to "lead the witness," they let Noah tell them what was troubling him: "Nobody plays with me, and some kids are mean." Eric's heart ached, too, as Noah cried.

"We are a month into a three-month quarter," Eric said to Rachel, "And we've paid for the full quarter. Would you agree to have Noah stay until Christmas break?"

Noah looked doubtful.

"What if I talk to the teacher about those kids ignoring you," Rachel asked.

Noah nodded: "Okay. But if I still don't like it, I won't have to stay?"

• • •

Eric and Rachel felt they had a fair compromise. Maybe Rachel had observed the school on a bad day. Maybe Noah would come to like it. As October yielded to November, however, little changed. Rachel began scouting other preschools. Noah had been shy since he was a baby.

Perhaps he would thrive in a smaller, less formal environment. As it turned out, Rachel found a more intimate daycare program. The owner was a friendly woman in her late thirties. Furthermore, the cost was a fraction of what the private preschool charged. The owner had three aides—one was a warm older woman and the others were in college studying to be teachers. When Rachel asked whether she could observe, the owner said: "Anytime, but I have one condition. If you stay for more than an hour, I'm putting you to work."

Every child is unique. Depending on their personalities, they may thrive in one environment and fail in another. The only way to find out what is best is to watch and learn. Not every school with a good reputation is the best fit for your child. If you have concerns, give our checklists a try.

Parents also need babysitters for the occasional night out or regular events that take you away from home. Babysitters can include grandparents, older siblings, aunts or uncles, teenagers, young adults, neighbors, and friends. Remember, not all babysitters, even if they are family members or friends, are qualified to care for your children.

## Peer Pressure

When your children are young, you are their most influential and, therefore, most important teacher. They hang on to your every word. *You're* the one they ask why the sky is blue. *You* have the power to vanquish monsters from the closet. *You* stand on a pedestal high above all others. Then one day, your little boy informs you that his best friend says there's no Santa Claus. Before long, the friend's word seems to hold as much weight as your own. You ask yourself: When did I suddenly begin competing for influence with a prepubescent know-it-all?

Sooner or later, all children start questioning their parents and listening more to their friends. The key is whether you have been teaching your children those all-important prosocial skills since they were old enough to learn to say please instead of "gimme." If you have done your part, the chances are good that your children will select friends who share similar sets of positive skills. Then, when your children's friends gain power, their influence will at least be more positive than negative.

Peer pressure is strong. Your children's friends are either your friends or your enemies. One delinquent peer can wipe out weeks of work to get your daughter to come home on time. To maintain your influence, you must guide your children toward meaningful friendships with children who play well with others and spend time in supervised activities that promote the development of prosocial skills like empathy, caring, sharing, taking turns, and cooperating with parents and teachers. Your mission is to expose your children to environments where the priority is on positive social skills.

Jacob, the boy who left the dinner table without permission to Skype with a friend, loves video games and he loves to Skype with friends while playing. His parents have established clear time limits, but sometimes they allow flexibility. In this scenario, we find Jacob at home with his dad on a college football Saturday afternoon. His mother was out with friends, so his dad gave Jacob extra time to play a video game with his friend Zach while he binge-watched games on half a dozen sports channels. While the cat's away...

 Jacob's dad muted the TV during a commercial to grab another slice of pizza and a coke from the kitchen. As he headed back to the living room, he paused to listen in on his son. As usual, Jacob was Skyping and playing. But what Robert heard coming from the den was confusing.

"Grab your sword and fight the horde, wiener," said an unfamiliar voice over the speaker amid ominous sound effects.

"Aye, my lord," Jacob answered.

"Let's kill them all. Mortal bastards!" The unfamiliar voice sounded older than Zach.

"Death awaits, ye," Jacob chimed in.

"Run him through. Spill his guts and drink his blood," the voice cackled.

Robert stepped inside the doorway to the den. He could see an older boy's face on the screen of the iPad.

"Hey! Watch my back, little dumbass."

Robert cleared his throat, prompting Jacob to jump. "Who are you Skyping with and what is that?" he asked. The computer screen displayed a group of monsters attacking a castle.

"Dad!" Jacob's eyes darted between the screen and his father.

"Where'd you go? They're going to kill us. Pick up your sword, turd!" the screen voice growled.

"Hey, sorry," Jacob said guiltily. "I gotta go."

"No way, laddie," said the voice.

Jacob disconnected from Skype and shut down the computer. He turned and smiled nervously at his dad.

• • •

All parents are tempted to allow kids extra freedom so they can enjoy their own adult pleasures. It is a reasonable thing to do, and honest parents admit to it on occasion. That is not the issue here. The problem is that Jacob took advantage of the situation, figuring (correctly) that his dad would be so involved in football games that he would never notice he was playing with someone other than his friend Zach. Robert used a commercial break to check on his son. Keeping his eyes and ears open, he discovered that Jacob had jumped the fence and ranged into new and inappropriate territories for a nine-year-old. Not only was he *not* playing a video game on his approved playlist; he was engaged in a violent game with an unfamiliar older boy who was being vulgar by Robert's standards. Robert was smart to put his football game on pause and gather information. Notice how he manages to stay calm and use his active listening skills to find out more about Jacob and his friends.

 "Jacob, who was that?" Robert asked in a neutral tone. He took a sip of his coke and waited.

"Uh, that's Teddy, Zach's older brother."

"Where's Zach?"

"He had to go somewhere with his mom."

Robert stood quietly, collecting his thoughts.

"Family meeting in five minutes. I'll be in the living room."

Jacob slumped in his chair, knowing he was busted. When he sat across from his father, he tried to act as if nothing unusual had happened.

"What game were you playing with this fellow Teddy? And how come I've never met Teddy?"

"He goes away to school. But he got to come back for the weekend."

"Uh-huh. And, let me ask again, what were you playing?"

Jacob mumbled the name of a video game not on the approved list. "It's okay, Dad. It's just like the other games, except you have to defend yourself with your team."

"So you and Teddy are on the same team?"

"Yeah. He's teaching me to play."

"Sounds like he's teaching you more than that. How old is he?"

"Um, fourteen. Zach said his brother needed someone to play with, so he let me use his account."

"Okay, Jacob. I didn't like what I heard coming out of Teddy's mouth. We need to establish some new rules."

Jacob shifted nervously in the chair and looked as if he were about to say something he would regret. Robert held up his hand: "Let me finish, son."

Robert did not want him playing violent games with Teddy, an older boy who had been sent away to school for some serious behavior issues.

"First, I'm guessing you knew I wouldn't approve of this game. From here on, I want you to talk to me before playing any new games over the Internet. Second, it is absolutely not cool to be playing with a fourteen-year-old without permission. You may not see it, but there's a very big difference between being nine and being old enough for high school. Last, I'm concerned that Zach may not be the best influence for you."

Several times, Robert had to regulate his emotions. He felt guilty for letting Jacob have too much time on his own; he was appalled at the level of violence, not only in the game, but in the language coming from this older boy. Rather than falling into a tirade, however, he calmly gathered information.

"But, Dad. Zach knows all the games. He's my friend."

"Do you hang out at school together?" Robert asked.

"Well, not really. Mostly we Skype and play video games."

"Do you have other friends you can play with?"

"Yes, but they don't get to play as much as Zach."

"Oh really?" Robert thought to himself: So I'm letting him play more than other parents and with a kid he doesn't hang out with at school. "Why don't you spend time with Zach at school?"

"I guess 'cause he's kind of a bully, but he's nice to me."

"Have you met Zach's parents?" Robert asked. Then he thought to himself: Have *I* met them?

"No. His dad is traveling most of the time, and his mom is always going out somewhere."

.   .   .

Notice how skillfully Robert followed the active listening technique and asked questions to find out more about Zach and his family. He kept his thoughts to himself and kept the questions neutral, so they didn't come across as an interrogation. He realized he knew next to nothing about the kid Jacob was spending hours with each week, and he knew even less about the family. He needed a plan to encourage Jacob to spend time with nine-year-old boys whose parents paid more attention.

Robert tried for some more information.

"Did Zach's brother get in trouble? Is that why he goes away to school?"

"He did something to the school's computers and had to go away," Jacob admitted reluctantly.

Robert mentally pegged Teddy as an unsupervised adolescent hacker—not the kind of kid he wanted influencing his son. "Does Zach get in trouble, too?"

"Um, well, sometimes for fighting and talking back to teachers."

Good lord, Robert thought. How did I let this happen? "Jacob, I want you to think about how kids behave around Zach and ask yourself if you want them to treat you like they do him. Look around at the kids you admire and the kids you don't admire and ask yourself what makes them different. Then ask yourself which group you want to be part of."

"But Dad," Jacob argued, "Zach won't have anyone else to play with. It would be mean for me to dump him."

"I understand. I don't want you to feel mean. Maybe we can invite Zach to come over when your mom or I are here. But I still want you to think hard about which group of kids you want to be part of," Robert said.

"Okay. Are you going to tell Mom?"

"Mom and I don't keep secrets," his dad reassured him. "But I can let her know that your intentions were good. We will work on a plan for you to spend more time with kids who don't get into trouble so much. Deal?"

"Yep. Deal, Dad."

"Okay. Come watch the end of the game with me. Then you have some chores to do."

• • •

Research shows that children are selective when it comes to choosing friends. The selection process begins as early as preschool and continues throughout life. Well-behaved children prefer to hang out with kids who follow rules, share, take turns, and cooperate. Aggressive kids tend to be rejected by well-behaved children, who don't like to play with kids who get in trouble and don't follow the rules. Poorly socialized children drift into groups with other kids with behavior problems, and the members of this peer group teach each other to lie, cheat, steal, or worse.

As your influence decreases, peer influence increases. It is not a question of whether it will happen. It is only a matter of when. If your children hang out with kids who get in trouble, they will be in trouble too—probably sooner rather than later. Our studies show that helping your children choose well-socialized peers when they are young is far easier than pulling them out of the wrong crowd as they grow older. The best way to ensure that your children fall in with a cooperative peer group is to teach them prosocial skills while you are still on that pedestal.

# Recap

The primary goal of monitoring your children is to keep them safe while facilitating their opportunities to grow and develop. We have to be watchful at home, in the neighborhood, with the Internet, at school or daycare, and with friends. The extent of monitoring each child needs has to be calibrated to their age, their level of functioning, how dependable they are, and the safety of the environments in which they live, work, and play. Your active listening and problem-solving skills will enable you to talk with your children and relevant adults to gather information, and regulating your emotions will help you stay calm when monitoring shows you that there may be a problem.

## *Practice Assignment*

Choose two activities that are most suitable for your monitoring needs.

- Make a list of names, addresses, and phone numbers of important people that may be needed in case of emergency. Post it in a place where it is easily found and program it into your phone. Examples include: yourself, your partner/ spouse, other responsible adults or caregivers, doctors, coaches, friends, children's friends, their parents, others.

- Teach your children how to dial 911. Teach them when it is appropriate to call.

🗂 Check on the availability of extracurricular activities that your children can enjoy during extended holidays, summer vacations, after school, etc. Take into account their interests and talents (recreation, sports, activities, lessons, camps). Are there scholarships that make them affordable?

## Warning Signs for Caregivers

⊘ *Unannounced drop-ins not allowed.* Once in a while, parents should drop by unexpectedly to observe standard procedures and get a better understanding of their children's experiences in the childcare setting.

⊘ *Continuing unhappiness.* If your children do not adjust to going to a care facility, find out what's wrong. Talk with the caregiver. Increase your visits to observe scheduled and unscheduled activities. Notice how staff respond to your child's experiences. If a visit makes you uncomfortable, drop in unexpectedly at different times.

⊘ *Sudden unhappiness.* If your child was doing well at childcare, but suddenly becomes unhappy, find out what has changed. Talk with the staff, other parents whose children attend, and your child. Use your best active listening skills.

⊘ *Lax or indifferent care.* Observe your child's and other children's experiences when you visit the facility. Are children left to wait for long times? Are they left to play alone indoors or outdoors? Do they receive careful and friendly supervision? What strategies does the staff use to engage children with each other?

⊘ *Excessive number of injuries.* Injuries will happen in the best of places, but take notice if your child or other children attending the facility have frequent or recurring accidents.

⊘ *Harsh, rude, or indifferent staff.* Observe how the staff treat your child and other children. They should be pleasant, attentive, and respectful to the children, you, and other adults.

⊘ *Insufficient toys or activities.* What kinds of engaging activities are planned for children? Are the toys and play equipment safe, clean, and interesting? Is TV the primary activity? Is cooperative play encouraged?

⊘ *Defensive caregiver.* When you ask for information or express concerns, caregivers should be happy to answer your questions, listen to your concerns, and discuss matters rationally without becoming upset. At the same time, it is important to seek information and express concerns in a manner that doesn't invite a defensive response.

⊘ *Uneasy feelings.* Even though you may not be able to identify a specific problem, if you continue to feel uneasy about the care, or if you lack confidence in the staff, begin looking for a new facility.

## Guide for Babysitters

☑ *Provide emergency information.* Post a list of telephone numbers. Include your cell, numbers of family members or close friends, your pediatrician, and other emergency contacts. Suggest 911 for emergencies.

☑ *Explain the rules.* Be straightforward about issues like telephone use, TV use, computer and video-game use, visitors, and food.

☑ *Provide written rules for your children.* Include media rules, bedtime, and the need to follow the babysitter's directions. Check up on their behavior when you return.

☑ *Discuss discipline.* Tell babysitters how you want them to handle misbehavior like hitting each other or the babysitter, refusal to follow directions, ignoring bedtime or other routines.

☑ *Don't expect housecleaning.* It is fair to expect babysitters to clean up any mess they make, but not any that was there before their arrival.

☑ *Plan simple meals.* Provide information about where supplies can be found and what food should be used. Make sure that meals will be easy to provide and clean up.

☑ *Pay a fair price.* Rates are charged according to the number and ages of children, time spent, and the going rate in your neighborhood.

☑ *Check the sitter's skills.* Check references with other families who have used the sitter's services. If the sitter is a teenager, know the sitter's parents. Pay the sitter to watch your children for an hour when you are home. Come home unexpectedly sometimes to see how things are going. If you feel uncomfortable for any reason, take action.

☑ *Don't use sitters with a history of troublesome behavior.* Leave your children in the hands of reliable people. Sitters who have problems with alcohol, drugs, the law, or have been abusive may teach your children things you don't want them to know.

☑ *Don't disregard past problems.* When leaving your children in the care of others, even family members, consider history. Some parents have told us that they were surprised that their uncle, friend, or other person was inappropriate with their child. The parents thought the individual would "know better" because they had had bad experiences themselves. Be watchful and err on the side of safety.

# Chapter Nine

# Teach Your Children Well

P at yourself on the back. Over the last eight chapters, you have honed a versatile set of parenting skills that you can now use to guide your children as they navigate their way from preschool to high school. In this chapter, we will focus on teaching good study habits and getting along with teachers, as well as strategies to troubleshoot problems. But first let's look at how the skills you have learned will help you better help your kids at school:

- *Setting goals* enables you to assess your children's progress in the classroom and address potential issues, like leaving for school on time, completing homework, and getting along with teachers and students.

- *Giving clear directions* increases your children's spirit of cooperation, which carries over to their interactions with classmates, teachers, and other adults.

- *Using encouragement* to teach new skills builds your children's self-confidence to address daily challenges at school. Extend the practice of catching your children being good at home to their study habits and the choices they make with peers in school and social settings.

*Regulating your emotions* improves your ability to troubleshoot problems your children encounter at school. You are the role model they will follow when dealing with their emotions.

*Setting limits* and providing consistent discipline teaches your children that their actions have predictable consequences. They have learned that positive behaviors generate rewards, while negative behaviors—not following directions in the classroom, failing to do or turn in homework, or being late for school—have sanctions. Remember that the way your children behave toward you generally carries over at school.

*Active listening* helps you discover how your children behave at school, the reasons a teacher sends home a note, or why your child comes home upset.

*Problem-solving* with family meetings engages children in decision-making about everything from resolving conflicts with classmates and teachers to choosing extracurricular activities.

You are your children's first and most important teacher. You are the one who teaches them how to organize their work, meet deadlines, fulfill responsibilities, and behave appropriately in structured settings. You ensure their school success by supporting strong study habits and monitoring their progress in their classes.

# Doing Well

Regardless of your specific values, it's safe to assume that we all share the goal of wanting our children to "do well" in school. But what does doing well in school mean to you and your individual children at the current stage in their school life? The best way to figure this out is to set up a meeting with your spouse or partner and discuss your goals.

Remember how Daniella and Cesar held a family meeting to settle the bathroom wars with Ava and her brothers? They apply the same approach at the beginning of each new school year to assess their children's individual progress and to update their goals. This year, Ava is entering the eighth grade, Benito the fifth, and Miguel the third. For their initial discussion, they chose to meet alone while their children were all away visiting friends.

"What do think Ava's biggest challenges will be this year?" Daniella asked.

"Socially she's fine," Cesar commented, "actually more than fine, and for that reason I suspect she'll have a hard time keeping her head focused on the books. You've noticed that boys are becoming a constant topic of conversation."

"I'm glad she prefers spending after-school time in groups of friends. She's already asking about dating. Her social life has interfered with her homework," Daniella paused and wrote down, "Attention to homework. Reward study skills" next to Ava's name.

"Benito's doing alright," Daniella continued. "He loves sports and he's with a good group of friends. He's making mostly Bs, but, remember, he was having trouble with math at the end of the last school year. I don't know whether the work was getting harder for him or if he was getting lazy. Either way, we need to watch his math." She added a note about it next to his name.

"I'll check with his teacher after a couple of weeks to see how he's doing," Cesar promised. "Can we afford a tutor if necessary? I have absolutely no understanding of Common Core math."

"Sure, if we need to. But let's see if we can help him apply himself," Daniella said.

"What do think of making some of the time he spends on sports contingent on improving his math grades?" Cesar asked.

Daniella shook her head. "I don't think so. He loves sports, he's really good at them, and his teammates are also his circle of friends. It would feel like punishment and that would make him hate math. Let's encourage him for focusing on his math homework."

Both parents agreed to continue supporting Benito's interest in sports while redesigning his incentive chart to encourage more time spent on math homework. They decided to let him pick some incentives for spending more time on math.

"And now we come to Miguel," Daniella said. "He's probably the smartest one in the family, but he has the worst grades. He was starting to get in trouble toward the end of the school year for cutting up in class."

"His teacher said he seemed bored most of the time and that probably contributed to his acting up," Cesar said, remembering the meeting he had had with Miguel's teacher the previous May.

"Frankly, I think he would benefit from a more challenging environment. But I know we can't afford private school. So...?" Daniella searched her husband's eyes.

Cesar rubbed his chin. "Do you think he would respond to an incentive chart for homework to get his grades up from mostly Cs to Bs?"

"I don't know. He's always been the hardest one to motivate with extra privileges," Daniella said. "I hate to say it, but I think Miguel will most likely respond to cash. If we offer money as an incentive, he might even get all As."

"You know people call that bribery," Cesar said.

"Maybe. But I don't care as long as it works," she said. "Besides, is it bribery when I get a bonus for bringing in new business for my firm? I like to think they call that rewarding good work. Bribes are promises made in exchange for dishonest deeds."

"OK," Cesar agreed, "but if we're going to offer cash for grades, then I think we need to help him do what it takes to get good grades—that means daily homework. How about giving him cash for grades each term?"

"Remember he's only eight," Daniella said, "so waiting until the end of a term will seem like a lifetime. Let's make the extra effort to give him a daily reward and take him to the bank each week to deposit his hard-earned cash."

Daniella summarized their strategy: "Okay. For Ava, we have to balance her social life with schoolwork. Spending time with her friends will be her incentive. For Benito, higher grades earn benefits related to sports. And for Miguel, our lazy genius, we'll see if he responds to cash for following a daily homework routine. We'll use these notes to create agreements with the kids at our family meeting next week. It looks like we'll have three incentive charts going for homework."

. . .

With common goals established between partners, it was time to follow up with a family meeting to discuss goals and expectations with the children. Daniella and Cesar held separate meetings with each child to give them a chance to shape the steps and select their own incentives.

Let us count the many ways that Daniella and Cesar put their parenting skills to work in their discussion:

☑ They wisely met alone to make a plan before bringing the kids in for a confab.

☑ They considered the individual strengths and challenges for each child separately.

☑ Even though they assessed each child separately, they discovered that all of their children would benefit from paying more attention to homework. Incentive charts will be their approach, with a tailored incentive system for each.

☑ They avoided a common mistake almost all parents make—use of a penalty system (for Benito for not making good grades) rather than an encouragement system for taking the steps necessary to achieve the goal.

☑ Another common mistake they avoided was providing one big incentive for end-of-term grades. This approach tends to fail unless the child is well-organized and self-motivated. The daily tracking approach requires parents to pay attention every day as their children practice the skill—that is a secret to success.

☑ Finally, they resolved their bribe versus reward controversy and accepted that it is OK to pay children to encourage success, realizing that they respond to motivators at work as well.

## Incentive Charts

Incentive charts work beautifully for dealing with homework issues. Here are examples of the charts that Daniella and Cesar developed for Ava (page 226) and Benito (page 227).

## Ava's Incentive Chart

| Name: Ava | | | | Week: | | | | |
|---|---|---|---|---|---|---|---|---|
| **Routine/task:**<br>**Homework** | **Points**<br>**10** | **Mon** | **Tues** | **Wed** | **Thurs** | **Fri** | **Sat** | **Sun** |
| **Step 1:**<br><br>Start within 60 min.<br>after dinner dishes | 2 | | | | | | | |
| **Step 2:**<br><br>Study at desk | 1 | | | | | | | |
| **Step 3:**<br><br>Study for 80 min.*<br>(1 point per 20 min) | 4 | | | | | | | |
| **Step 4:**<br><br>No TV, screen time,<br>or texting unless for<br>homework | 2 | | | | | | | |
| **Step 5:**<br><br>Show work to parent | 1 | | | | | | | |
| **Daily Total:** | 10 | | | | | | | |

*Bonus points for each additional 20 minutes.*

| Total points needed: | 7 | **Review time:** Before Bed |
|---|---|---|
| Possible Incentives: | | 60 min extra social time • 60 min extra screen time • 50¢ a point |

# Benito's Incentive Chart

| Name: Benito | | | | | Week: | | | | |
|---|---|---|---|---|---|---|---|---|---|
| **Routine/task:** **Homework** | **Points** **10** | **Mon** | **Tues** | **Wed** | **Thurs** | **Fri** | **Sat** | **Sun** | |
| **Step 1:** Start within 15 min. after dinner dishes | 2 | | | | | | | | |
| **Step 2:** Organize books and school materials | 2 | | | | | | | | |
| **Step 3:** Start with math— 20 min | 2 | | | | | | | | |
| **Step 4:** Follow with other homework—30 min | 2 | | | | | | | | |
| **Step 5:** Show work to parent | 2 | | | | | | | | |
| **Daily Total:** | 10 | | | | | | | | |

| Total points needed: | 7 | **Review time:** End of study period |
|---|---|---|
| Possible Incentives: | | Screen time • Sports time with Dad • 50¢ a point up to $10 a week |

## Ava

When Daniella and Cesar met with Ava to negotiate her homework plan, they started by talking about the things she already does well. For example, she regularly spends a minimum of thirty to forty minutes on homework. She keeps her work organized and tidy. However, in many school systems (including this family's), the rule of thumb is about ten minutes of daily homework for each year in school. As an eighth grader, Ava needs to double her study time to eighty minutes.

Ava often interrupts study time texting and chatting with friends, so she now earns points for staying focused and waiting until she's finished to contact her friends. Sometimes, Ava spends extra time on homework for special projects or tests, so she negotiated bonus points. Ava said she wanted to earn more social time and screen time, and to trade in points for money. Usually, we recommend that parents not assign four points to a single step on a chart, because failure to do that one step precludes success for the whole day. However, because Ava always does at least thirty minutes of homework, they decided to try this out.

You can be flexible and set up the charts for your children in whatever way works best for them and for you.

Benito's chart came next. Notice the similarities and differences in the steps, points, and incentives between his chart and Ava's.

## Benito

Benito's main issue is organization. His backpack is something of a catastrophe. All sorts of things are crammed in there—schoolwork, sports equipment, dirty socks, whatever. He agreed he needed help after Ava hid a cheeseburger in his backpack for almost a week. It fell out of his pack in class.

Daniella and Cesar agreed that Benito needed to work on organizing his school materials every day. Cesar spent the first evening helping him straighten things out to set him up for success. They agreed that he would do math first to get it out of the way, and then he could do other homework that he disliked less. He chose extra screen time and time to play sports with Dad—and of course, the money—as his incentives. His parents decided to set a limit on the money the boys could earn each week, although not so for Ava because she is older (and would probably prefer social time).

## Productive Learning Environments

As you think about ways to bolster your children's success at school, there are many things to consider. Do they bring home assignment sheets with teachers' expectations and due dates? Do you review the assignment sheets? Are their notebooks or school folders well organized? When is study time? Does it follow a particular activity (after snack, after school, after dinner dishes)? Or, does it come before recreational activities (before screen time, texting, or going out to play)? What kind of environment have you established for homework activities? Is the place quiet, without distractions, with good lighting and necessary materials? Do your children stay in the study place for the allotted time? Do they interrupt their work to answer calls, text, check out something on TV? Do they make progress on their work? Do you check in with them? Are you encouraging?

Your skills using an incentive chart transfer beautifully to helping children establish homework routines. Some children need very little encouragement, while others come up with a thousand distractions and excuses to avoid the work. With incentive charts, you can identify problems your children may be facing and break them into achievable steps. It's also important to check in with teachers so you understand their expectations.

We cannot emphasize enough your role as your children's *first and most important teachers*. You have been shaping their verbal and physical development from day one. Studies show that how much you talk to your children and the way you talk to them (even when they are babies) shapes their language skills, affecting the number of words in their vocabulary and their speech patterns. These patterns persist as your children enter preschool, elementary school, and other social settings. Your attitudes about education also affect how your children view school. If you treat school as an amazing childhood adventure, chances are good that your children will too.

You communicate your attitudes toward school through your behavior as a parent. How you talk about school when you are around your children and what they hear you talk about when you think they aren't listening also shape their attitudes. How often you make time to attend school plays, science fairs, and other activities tells your children how much you care about them and their academic progress.

You also show your level of interest and involvement through family meetings. They provide ideal opportunities for role play. For example, one parent can take the part of the child getting ready in the morning (if you're developing an organizing routine or checklist) and the other can play the parent encouraging the child, which models how the activity will take place. Then you can switch and let the child play the role of child and practice the routine. It's important to make these little role plays fun.

Finally, remember to discuss your expectations. Common topics you may want to address include:

- ☑ Routines for bedtime on school nights to prepare for the morning rush. This may mean selecting and laying out clothes or other school necessities.

- ☑ Routines for morning activities that prevent chaos and promote leaving on time.

- ☑ Routines for "brain training," "power reading," and homework.

# Brain Training

The brain is like a muscle that you can strengthen with exercise. You can help your children build brainpower with regular brain-training sessions. Like any muscle, the brain needs repetitive exercise to build strength. Make brain training fun and playful, just as you try to do with your own physical workouts. Remember to accentuate the positive and provide your children with plenty of encouragement. For school-age children, homework or other academic skills can be the focus of brain-training time. Preschoolers benefit from activities like coloring, looking at books, and building with blocks.

During extended holiday times, school-age children can shift brain-training activities from schoolwork to other types of development, like music, sports, or other skills. Plan activities that will pique the interests of each child based on age and developmental stage. Choose activities that reflect your values and your children's talents. The families we work with identify all kinds of activities for this exercise, including reading, drawing, listening to or making music, singing, storytelling, gardening, and writing. During brain-training time, take a break from your own activities and pay attention to your children, offering them encouragement and guidance if requested. They will develop expertise from consistent practice. It's not just the equipment you're born with that matters; it's how you develop your talents and interests.

Adjust workouts according to children's ages and attention spans, and keep them relatively short. Be sure to make the practice routine. Brain-training strategies are similar to those that athletes follow. For example, successful exercise for both muscles and brains starts at present strength, or baseline, and gradually increases with daily workouts. Let's say you want to run in a marathon next year, but, at the moment, you can barely finish a mile. You will need to build strength in your legs and aerobic capacity in your lungs gradually. If you train regularly, there's no reason you cannot finish a marathon next year—or maybe a 10K.

The effects of brain training accumulate over the years and produce amazing results. Brain training is particularly valuable for children with attention challenges. For them, start with a very short period of time and gradually increase. Parents with children with attention deficit hyperactivity disorder (ADHD) who have used this exercise often report that their children increase their attention span and sometimes the ADHD improves.

## Strategies for Brain Training

- ⌂ Structure family routines to make brain training a priority.

- ⌂ Set a regular time. Daily routines establish habits.

- ⌂ Pick a time when your children function well. Daylight hours are best for most people. Plan alternative times when special events interfere with the schedule.

- ⌂ Train for a regular amount of time.

- ⌂ Start small for success. For most early elementary school children, a reasonable amount of time starts at fifteen minutes. Some children with high activity levels or attention problems may need to start at five or ten minutes.

- ⌂ Set a timer.

- ⌂ Gradually increase time and/or level of difficulty.

- ⌂ Provide a good setting. Set up a quiet place with good lighting and a clear working space with the necessary materials (paper, pencils, or books).

- ⌂ Use the same place every day. Routine trains the brain to get right to work.

- ⌂ Don't let phone calls, TV, games, texts, or chaos interfere.

- ⌂ Hold workouts five days a week. Daily brain training builds self-discipline and increases attention span.

- ⌂ Be present. Children need guidance and encouragement.

- ⌂ Pleasantly offer assistance when requested.

- ⌂ Praise your children's efforts.

- ⌂ Keep track of progress.

# Power Reading

Literacy—reading and writing—is one of the most basic academic skills. You probably already know that it is important to read aloud to your children. Sharing time together with books—apart from routine homework assignments—enhances children's vocabulary and helps them focus attention. As your children develop their own reading skills, take turns reading to each other in five- or ten-minute spurts. Have fun dramatizing storylines. Help them over difficult words. Avoid interrupting them with corrections; review problem words later. You will enhance their interest and comprehension if you engage them in discussions about what is happening in the story. By the way, simply reading around your children makes it more likely that they will pick up the habit. Try to engage in power reading daily, at about the same time each day. Reading at bedtime is a common example.

Build up a good supply of reading materials. The local library is an important resource, as are garage sales, thrift or secondhand stores, and neighborhood exchanges. Studies show that even little babies benefit when you read aloud to them. Here are some suggestions for strengthening the effect of reading with your children.

## Strategies for Power Reading

- *Gather books.* Find books that reflect your children's interests, your own interests, and interests you want to encourage.

- *Match age and abilities.* Fit material to each child's skill and level of development.

- *Get cozy.* Read when things are calm and in places where you can connect. Pleasant atmospheres will help your children associate books with comfort.

- *Engage prereaders.* Find stimulating picture books. Ask children to name things (colors, shapes, activities, feelings).

Repeat what they say to let them know you're listening and shape their pronunciation. Point out details of interest. Invite them to share their ideas about the story, which helps them develop communication skills.

*Encourage early readers.* Find books with easy words and pictures that help tell the story. Encourage them to sound out words or learn to recognize familiar words (cat, ball).

*Support developing readers.* Take turns reading. You read for five or ten minutes, then let your child read. Help them sound out difficult words. Avoid interrupting their flow with corrections. Come back to problem words or ideas later.

*Make it fun.* Dramatize while reading. To increase comprehension, ask questions about the story and what they think about it.

*Read often.* Make reading a priority in the family.

## Stumbling Blocks

Now let's dive deeper. Remember the stumbling blocks we discussed in chapter 3? In that context, we talked about barriers that interfere with completing a basic routine like going to bed on time. In the example, the challenge was the bathroom routine. We addressed the problem by breaking that routine into smaller steps. Stumbling blocks can disrupt a child's school progress in the same way. The task for parents is to identify stumbling blocks for each child and break them down into manageable steps.

Depending on the schools your children attend and the various philosophies teachers have, you may encounter homework issues as early as first grade. If you initiate brain training before your children start school, you can fit homework routines right into that format, with a few adjustments. During brain-training time for preschoolers, the older children can focus on schoolwork. Parents can promote good study habits by planning family activities to support the homework routine.

Again, just as with brain training, make sure the homework setting supports good study habits. The place should be quiet, with good lighting and a clear work space. The necessary materials need to be handy (paper, pencils, books). Using the same place every day trains the brain to get right to work. Establish a regular study time and place, stipulate a minimum amount of study time, and schedule schoolwork five days a week (even without specific assignments). Here is a checklist that can help you evaluate your child's study skills.

## *Student Study Skills Checklist*

- ☑ Brings home school notebook or folder
- ☑ Keeps notebook organized
- ☑ Brings home assignment sheet that describes activity and due date
- ☑ Shows assignment sheet to parent(s)
- ☑ Has a regular study time (Start and finish times _____)
- ☑ Starts studying on time
- ☑ Completes full study time
- ☑ Studies at a designated space
- ☑ Uses good study space: without distractions, good lighting, with necessary materials
- ☑ Makes progress during study time

Here is a checklist that can help you evaluate your support for good study skills.

## Parent Study Skills Checklist

- ☑ Do I provide a good study place?

- ☑ Do I support study time by clearing the deck of other activities?

- ☑ Do I check in with my child regarding assignments?

- ☑ Do I provide encouragement and guidance as requested?

- ☑ Do I provide incentives as earned?

. . .

Raising cooperative children is a long journey. Getting a good education is an ambitious goal that involves traveling a long course over many years. The education highway is filled with roadblocks, detours, and sometimes even land mines. You can help your children by identifying stumbling blocks that interfere with their success. Remember that the best way to teach children is through encouragement as they take the many small steps that lead to achieving a goal. Replace your nagging and criticism with encouragement.

In the figure on page 237, you see a child taking the journey to school success. First pay attention to the academic strengths this child already has: regular attendance, pays attention in class, follows directions, and completes class assignments. This child's stumbling block involves homework. His parents need to encourage him as he develops some new habits.

Whatever the stumbling block is for your child, take note, consider it a challenge instead of a problem, and figure out how to break it into steps small enough that your child can manage them. And, of course, remember that incentives motivate children when they are learning new routines or developing good habits. Incentive charts help structure ways

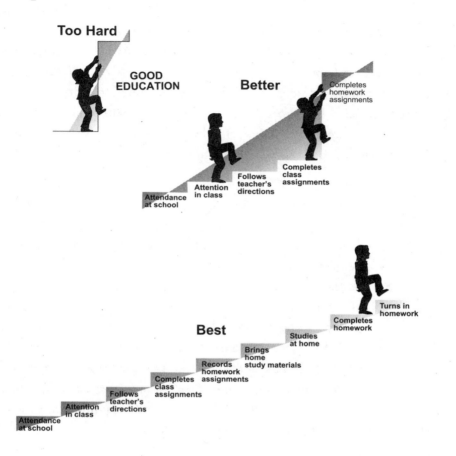

to motivate children as they take small steps on the path to academic success. The structure provided by incentive charts helps them learn to develop self-discipline.

# Changes in Family Dynamics

We have stressed throughout this book the importance of parenting your children through the many changes in family life. Next to school transitions, one of the most significant changes that families experience is separation and divorce. Routines that worked well when the family was together may no longer be possible under the new family dynamic. One of the things that suffers during a divorce may be your children's grades.

In chapter 3, we met Stacey and Steven, whose eleven-year-old son James' grades began to tank when they separated. When they discovered that James was not doing his homework, they realized they needed to establish a new routine. James had been accustomed to doing his homework after school. Mom was at home to provide structure, and James was motivated to complete his schoolwork by the promise of throwing a football with his dad when he came home from work.

After his parents' divorce, James lost interest in homework because the payoff was removed—playing with his dad in the evening. Stacey's new job meant she was no longer at home after school. So she had to design a new routine. She changed the time for homework from after school to immediately after dinner when she could be there. After James finished his homework, he was allowed to read, play video games, or watch TV. Stacey picked up a nice, but inexpensive, desk from a yard sale and created a good study space for James. She made sure that he started homework at a regular time each evening and that he worked at it for thirty minutes. She made herself available to help him deal with any problems.

James was good at most of his subjects, but he found science boring. Stacey made sure that he started his homework with science and followed it up with something he found easier. Just before bedtime, she spent fifteen minutes reading with him. She let him pick what they would read and discuss. He often chose *Sports Illustrated*, his favorite magazine. Stacey would have preferred to read fiction, but she wanted to share in James' interests.

Over time, Stacey enjoyed reading sports articles with him. She learned more about college football and NCAA basketball than she could have imagined. Her new expertise provided an entry into her son's world and she could hold her own in a conversation over dinner about who would become the next first-round draft choices in the NFL. The important point is that she chose a topic that interested James, which made the routine fun for him.

• • •

Stacey used a clever trick that we use in our personal lives called the Premack Principle, which states simply that you do an unpleasant activity first and follow it up with something you like better. This keeps you from dreading the thing you like least, because you get it done from the outset. This works well for procrastinators.

When establishing homework routines, parents first provide the necessary guidance and support to help their children develop study skills, often with the use of an incentive chart and checklists. To complete homework, children need to be able to organize materials, follow study routines, complete assignments on time, and turn them in dependably. Parents can pave the way by designing a study plan, helping their children get started, breaking stumbling blocks into achievable steps, and encouraging progress. The important thing is to begin wherever your children are in the learning process and help them week by week, year by year. As parents, we impose a certain amount of discipline to help our children develop good learning habits. Eventually, they learn self-discipline. Don't expect your children to run a marathon their first day on the track.

# Linking Home and School

It is important for parents to use strategies for effectively communicating with school personnel, teachers, counselors, and other adults who work with their children in the school environment. Most parents are busy and wish they had more time to be involved with school. Often, however, outside of parent-teacher conferences and the occasional school play, we have pretty limited contact with teachers and the parents of classmates.

Transitions—moving, having a new child, divorce or repartnering, changing schools—are times when children need more structure, yet parents are often distracted with their own issues. It is not uncommon for parents' first involvement with schools to be related to some type of problem.

Because school is such an important part of your children's lives, you want to know about their school experiences. When you are involved in their activities, you can watch them develop skills, interact with their classmates, and learn to work and play cooperatively with others. Teachers are busy and so are parents. If you make time to establish a relationship with teachers when there are no problems, you will be in a good position to collaborate to help your children if they occur.

Your active listening skills will be handy when you meet with teachers to find out about your children's lives at school. Your contact with teachers should be based, in part, on how well your children are doing, or special concerns that may develop in the course of the year (illnesses, traumas, transitions, celebrations). Many parents are surprised to learn that some children who behave well at home have behavior problems at school. On the other hand, some children who are troublesome at home are well-behaved at school. And there are those who do well or poorly in both settings.

Before you meet your children's teachers, do some homework of your own. Your first assignment is to discover what you already know about your children's school life, and then learn what you need to know. How many of these important facts do you know?

## Do I Know?

- ☑ The school secretary's name
- ☑ The school nurse's name
- ☑ The teacher's name
- ☑ The principal's name

☑ The number of children in class

☑ The schedule of daily activities

☑ Where my child sits in the classroom

☑ Where my child eats lunch

☑ What time my child has recess

☑ My child's favorite subject

☑ My child's least favorite subject

☑ If my child volunteers to answer questions in class

☑ What my child does when confused

☑ What problems my child has with classmates

☑ What my child does if upset by a classmate

The following are common situations that can make a parent-teacher conference necessary. Consider the examples and imagine using your integrated set of parenting tools to address each one. Remember to listen carefully to what the teacher has to say, keep your mind open, regulate your emotions, know that you and your children's teachers are on the same side, and use the full set of problem-solving strategies.

☑ Your child says he/she never has homework, but your neighbor's child, who has the same teacher, has homework every day. You want to talk to the teacher, but the last time you did, you got the feeling he thought of you as a rotten parent.

☑ You received a note from school saying your child has been absent for several days. As far as you know, she hasn't missed a minute of school.

☑ You and your middle-school-age child are frustrated with his homework. There's too much and it's too hard. You want to talk to his teacher.

☑ The vice-principal calls to tell you your child was in detention today for calling the substitute teacher names and refusing to follow directions.

☑ The preschool teacher tells you that your three-year-old bit another child and that child's parent wants your child removed from the school.

☑ The teacher reports that your child stole some pencils from the classroom supplies.

# Recap

The journey leading to a "good education"—whatever that may be—has many challenges. As your children's most important teachers, you can smooth the way by anticipating and preventing problems along the way. Connecting with key people at school enables you to track your children's life at school. Incentive charts and checklists tailored to school issues can keep everyone on track. Prioritizing brain training and power reading gives your children a head start.

Pay special attention to transitions when routines tend to fall apart. The beginning and end of the school year are common stressors for children. A family illness, moving to a new city or school district, fighting with your spouse in front of the children, or a divorce or repartnering can affect your children's performance. If you know that a major change is coming, prepare your children to soften the impact. Remember, no matter what, you have the skills to survive rough patches and to make your children's experience of school one of wonder and adventure.

## Practice Assignment

Choose one or two of the following activities. Take into consideration the age of your child and particular situations you want to address.

- *Establish a fifteen-minute brain-training time.* Make a plan for the kinds of activities your children can do during that time. Take into account their different ages and skill levels.

- *Create an incentive chart for school.* Set a goal for improving your child's school readiness. Your choice may be leaving for school on time, brain-training time, homework, or power reading. Involve your children in making the choice.

- *Develop a checklist.* Help your children get organized by creating a checklist of things that need to be done each day for school. For example, what do your children need in their backpacks before leaving home?

- *Use your problem-solving skills to address a school issue.* Is there a behavior you want to encourage, enhance, or discourage? Some areas to address include time management, procrastination, and controlling emotions in particular situations. Follow the problem-solving technique.

- *Communicate with your children's teachers.* Make contact with a teacher to find out about your child's experience at school. One choice is to call, email, or text the teacher asking for a time to talk. Things to ask about include special activities coming up or recently past, your child's progress in general or with regard to something specific, and questions about homework.

# Chapter Ten

# United We Stand

Some children are adept at using the "divide and conquer" approach with their parents to get their way. Jerry calls this classic ploy the "sadomasochistic arabesque," a dance requiring at least three partners. The parents never dance with each other; instead, each dances separately with one of the children. When this happens, the abandoned partner tries to stop the music. Each parent's relationship to the child is delicately balanced. One occupies the role of harsh disciplinarian who punishes problem behaviors and brings the child's behavior under moderate control. The other attempts to balance the martinet's severity by being warm and permissive, no matter how the children behave. As a result, when the disciplinarian is away, the child's behavior is out of control. From the despairing despot's perspective, the child is fine when he or she is present; the other parent is just too *laissez-faire* or permissive. The child, an active participant in the arabesque, knows just how to exploit the rift between the parents.

There are many variations on this theme. Divorced families and stepfamilies are especially vulnerable. Adults with the primary responsibility for raising children are bound to have different perspectives that require negotiation. When the adults work together as a united front, however, they can prevent children from hijacking the family dynamic and pitting one parent against the other.

A united parenting front is your strongest defense against this complex dance. In the following example, we take a look at a couple who are learning to create a blended family—a daunting challenge for any new couple. The only way they will survive is to stand together and make no assumptions about what the other is thinking. They need to draw upon all of the skills we have discussed so far.

# The End Run

Kim and John have a blended family with three boys—John's sons eleven-year-old Marcus and nine-year-old Brent, and Kim's son ten-year-old Aiden. John has shared custody of his sons, keeping them every other week and weekend; Kim has primary custody of Aiden, so he is with the new blended family all but two weekends a month. The couple initially considered it a stroke of luck that they had sons so close in age and with the same interests. However, the strong bond between the boys also presented challenges early in the marriage.

The couple soon found themselves arguing over differences in child-rearing philosophies within earshot of the boys. Kim thought that John was too lax, and, of course, John considered Kim's parenting style too strict. Their most recent conflict is centered on the children's bedtimes. The routine for Aiden is bedtime at 8:30 on school nights and 9:30 on Fridays and Saturdays. John had been more lax when he was living alone with his boys after his divorce, setting a 9:00 bedtime on school nights and letting them stay up as late as they wanted on weekends.

Before the wedding, Kim was flexible about letting her son stay up later with John's boys when the families were together on weekends. She assumed John's boys would conform to her bedtime rules after they moved in together. That was not to be. John agreed to the earlier bedtime on school nights, because his boys had trouble getting up in the morning. But weekend bedtimes were a struggle for the couple. John's boys enlisted Aiden in conspiracies to stay up as late as possible, and they discovered that John caved in easily. This dynamic generated conflict between the parents when the three boys sided against Kim and recruited John to their side. When Kim stood her ground, she felt that John's boys viewed her as the wicked step-mother—a perception she worked hard to avoid.

Kim was surprised and hurt when John took sides with the boys. When she complained that the boys were plotting against her, John told her she was overreacting and tried to reassure her that the boys would come around to "her ways" once everyone was settled into their new family. Kim argued it was their responsibility as parents to design the family they wanted and not leave it to the boys. Without a clear goal that they both agreed on, these parents of a newly blended family were foundering, like a ship without a rudder.

 One Friday evening, Kim and John were putting away the dinner dishes when Kim paused and tilted her head: "Do you hear that?"

John listened for a few moments and shook his head. "Hmm. Nope."

"Exactly," Kim said. "Three boys under one roof and not a peep?" She put her finger to her lips and motioned John to follow her. They tiptoed down the hallway toward the family room. As they neared the half-shut door, they heard the boys' muffled voices. Kim and John stood quietly in the hallway and listened.

"Sorry Aiden, but your mom's bedtime rules suck, especially when it's the weekend and we don't have to get up for school," Marcus said. "So when we finish watching their movie, I'll get my dad to give us cookies and milk. Aiden, while I'm in the kitchen, you beg your mom to let us play one video game before bed. Tell her how nice we've been to watch their show with them. Then they'll probably get bored and go to bed, and we can stay up as long we want. Brent, you stay with Aiden and say "pretty-please" and that kind of stuff. Got it?"

The boys chuckled and gave each other high fives. Kim seethed, while John suppressed a grin. She felt even more frustrated as they returned to the kitchen and sat down at the table. Kim whispered: "Do you see now? This is what I've been trying to tell you. That's why you have to stick with me or they'll be running the household."

"Wow. They think they've got us figured out, don't they," John admitted. "Divide and conquer. But don't all kids do that? I certainly did when I was their age."

Kim shook her head in disbelief. "Yes, I think most kids try to play their parents against each other, especially step-parents. But that doesn't mean we let them get away with it. It's our job to set the rules and stick by them. Look John, you know it isn't fair to have separate bedtimes or have different rules of any kind for that matter. I know I'm a good mother and I firmly believe that children need to stick with a routine. You agreed to the 8:30 bedtime on school nights and that's made it easier to get the boys up and out the door on time. Why can't we stick together on weekends too?"

"You were right about school nights, but I don't see the big deal on weekends. I think 9:30 is too early on a weekend night. They don't have to get up early, and if they sleep in, then so can we." John tried to flirt, but Kim held her ground.

"Your rule is basically no rule. Bedtime is whenever they drop off to sleep. They're a little young for that. We need to stick together. We're on the same team, remember?" Kim said.

"I still don't understand why you have to be so strict. I only get my sons every other week. What would it hurt to let the kids stay up together, at least on weekends?"

Kim felt exasperated. She couldn't understand why he didn't get it. "Please, John. Promise you'll stick by me tonight when I say it's time for bed at 9:30. As long as we let them get away with this, they'll keep doing it."

John heard the desperation in his wife's voice, so he agreed, mostly to placate her. Kim thought they had made progress. But when they finished the movie later and Marcus, on cue, asked for cookies and milk, John started laughing. He turned to Aiden and said: "And I bet you think we should let you boys stay up and play a video game."

John paused and looked as if he might support his wife. Then he opened his mouth and blew whatever chances he had left of finishing the night peacefully. "Honey, video games sound so boring. We might as well go on to bed," he said laughing.

Kim glared. She realized John didn't care about the weekend bedtime issue and was not going to support her. She felt alone. She stood up, brushing microwave popcorn from her lap. "Okay, why don't you stay up with the boys all night! You can even bunk on the floor in their room. And when you all drag yourselves out of bed or off the floor at noon tomorrow, you can figure out what you want to do with whatever's left of your day. I'll probably be at the gym. Or maybe I'll drive into the city with a friend. It's 9:30, and I'm going to bed now."

• • •

This kind of scenario plays out all too often in step-families. The conflict issue varies—it may be bedtime, hairstyles, table manners, you name it. The problem comes from long-standing values and routines that the two partners bring to the relationship and try to integrate into their new lifestyle. As an uninvolved bystander, it's not hard to see each parent's point of view. Kim's established routine worked well when her family consisted of her and Aiden. Now she is outnumbered. John and his sons have been living a less-structured lifestyle. When his boys enlist her son to their side, they overwhelm her. Most people reading this scenario, however, will agree that John blew it when he didn't keep his word and sided with the boys.

Even though John is sympathetic with the kids' point of view, he wants a pleasant evening with his wife and he knows both sides are going to have to give. So far, he has already moved in her direction with an earlier bedtime on school nights, and that has worked out well. Now, Kim may have to yield some as well. Further negotiation about bedtime is in this couple's future, but not now in front of the kids and not in a stressful situation when someone's angry. A better time to resolve their differences is when they are alone and enjoying each other's company. So, until that time, let's rewind and see how John could have played it better.

 When the family finishes watching the movie, Marcus, on cue, asks for cookies and milk. John starts laughing. He turns to Kim and smiles conspiratorially, puts his arm around her, looks Marcus in the eye, and says: "And I bet you think we should let you boys stay up and play a video game."

Marcus looks as if he has been caught with his hand in the cookie jar. "Ah, no."

"Good, because tonight you boys are going to bed at 9:30. If you do a good job tonight, we may continue this discussion about weekend bedtimes another time. First, you need to show us that you do as we tell you."

• • •

John was sorely tempted, and he has plans to convince Kim to lighten up. He loves his wife and wants this new family to work. Kim, ecstatic with John's support, feels herself loosening up, just a little. To create a stronger united parenting front—one that will clearly communicate to the boys that their divide-and-conquer schemes are futile—Kim and John plan a weekend alone together.

This couple enjoys camping and finds that the time spent alone together in the mountains is romantic, relaxing, and restorative. From past experience, they know that it's a perfect time to communicate. The first day and evening, they avoid talking about family or work and focus on each other. They know discussing problems is more productive after they've had a chance to remember why they love each other's company.

The next morning, sitting by the campfire after breakfast, they gazed out at the lake and snuggled closely for warmth. They had agreed ahead of time on a shared goal to resolve the boys' weekend bedtime issue. Kim began the conversation.

"I've been giving this a lot of thought," she said, "and I'm sure we can overcome this issue. I'd like the boys to have a reasonable bedtime, but I realize that I haven't explained why, and I'll bet you can't guess." Kim paused, giving John time to think.

"To be honest, I don't really get it. Why is it so important to you?" John asked with genuine interest.

"I had to ask myself the same question, and I finally figured it out. I was hoping that we would design our weekends for high-quality family time. When we let the boys stay up late, they sleep until noon the next day. That kind of blows the day. It's hard to do something fun together when half the day is already gone. It makes me worry that we're letting the opportunity to bond as a family slip through our fingers. I want weekends to be time for play as a family. I've never been able to experience that before. My ex was a workaholic and always left me and Aiden to fend for ourselves."

John looked surprised. "Well, I work so hard during the week that weekends for me—before I met you—represented a time to rest." He sipped his coffee, realizing that something about what he had said did not ring true. "I never realized this until now," he admitted, "but I got in the habit of staying up late with the boys so I would have an excuse to avoid doing things with my ex. She always had a list of a hundred chores and errands for me to do on weekends. She certainly did not want to do fun things with me and the boys. Staying up late meant sleeping in and delaying the endless chores."

John fell silent thinking about what he had just said. "So, let me see if I have this right. The reason you're so adamant about weekend bedtimes is because you want us to do fun things together as a family. It's not because you have chores for me and the boys to do as soon as we get up?" John visibly brightened. "Why didn't you tell me before?"

"I'm just now realizing my own motivation for wanting you and *our* boys up and ready to enjoy the weekend. I guess we needed to get away for a camping trip sooner," Kim said, giving her husband a hug. "The boys didn't know either. They're just being kids and wanting what they want in the moment. Whether we realized it or not, they were just following our leads. I think when we explain our plan—that weekends are fun family time—they will be more than happy to get to bed."

"I think I actually understand," John said. "How about a compromise? I still think 9:30 is a little early for a weekend night. How about we set bedtime on Friday and Saturday at 10:30 and keep that firm. That is—in bed, lights out, no talking. The extra hour gives them a little freedom, but it's not so late that everyone will be exhausted the next morning. What do you think?"

Kim smiled again at John. "I think that's a fair compromise. Let's shake on it."

· · ·

## The Huddle

Step-families tend to run into conflicts when establishing new routines, and for good reason. Each family enters the relationship with a different set of rules and rituals. Whether we realize it or not, we bring baggage loaded with assumptions and preconceptions based on our experiences. Those differences need to be identified and compromises negotiated between the parents, and not in the presence of the children. It is an unfortunate fact that children can smell conflict in the air, which provides them the opportunity to drive a wedge between their parents.

When John sided with the boys rather than his wife, a small crack in the couple's relationship got wider. The boys—and John—won a later bedtime and John gained the boys' gratitude. But at what cost to the parents' mutual trust and intimacy! The situation is like the safety protocol on airplanes. Adults are told to place the oxygen mask on themselves first so they can better attend to their children. United parenting is like that. In the rewind scenario, when John stood by his wife even though he disagreed with her point of view, he made it possible for them to negotiate a compromise later, when they could better share each other's perspectives.

When conflict between two parents comes into play, it's time to remember what you love about your partner. This couple loves outdoor activities, so they decided to work on their conflict on a camping trip alone together. That, by the way, is one of the advantages some step-families have—the children spend time with their other parent, which allows the custodial parent time for play. Kim and John scheduled a weekend camping trip and set the stage for effective problem-solving by waiting to talk until they had spent loving time together. One of the hardest, but most important, things to remember as a couple is to create a positive setting in which to discuss problems. When people are in a good mood, they think more creatively.

Kim opened the problem-solving discussion with an empowering statement: I believe we can overcome this issue. Then she stated her goal: I'd like the boys to have a reasonable bedtime. Next, she accepted some responsibility for the problem by acknowledging that she hadn't shared her rationale—she wants everyone to be up and ready for fun family time on the weekends. Notice that she invited John's perspective and paused to give him a chance to present his point of view. Kim's goal of having the family share fun activities on weekends was a shocker for John. His experience with his previous wife was that weekends were for household duties, certainly not for enjoyment. Once he saw the potential for this plan, he was more open to the earlier bedtime. After all, he too wants to play on weekends.

The next step that helped this couple was Kim's willingness to compromise by extending bedtime by an hour. John wisely added reassuring details—in bed, lights out, no talking. Of course, enforcing this new rule will present another issue for the couple to face, but for now, they have taken giant strides toward building a family lifestyle agreeable to both of them.

Now they must call a family meeting to engage the boys in the decision.

Kim and John set the family meeting for the following Thursday. That way, the new agreement would be fresh in the boys' minds on Friday when the the new bedtime rule went into effect. Kim liked to use a whiteboard and colored markers in family meetings, believing the visuals helped keep the boys' attention.

"Boys, I want you to memorize this number," Kim said, as she wrote 10:30 on the whiteboard. "Does anyone know what this is?"

The boys looked each other and shrugged. "This is your new weekend bedtime!"

The boys groaned and all looked directly at John, anticipating his intervention. John stood next to Kim and put his arm around her. "That's right, boys. From now on, weekend bedtime is 10:30. Lights out. No talking. No exceptions."

The boys groaned and fussed, but Kim and John kept standing together. Kim took the next step. She drew a circle around 10:30 with an arrow running from it. "Can anyone tell me why we are setting 10:30 as the new and improved bedtime?"

Marcus raised a hand. His mischievous look signaled that he was about to say something stupid. "Because you're mean?" The boys snickered. To their surprise, Kim wrote down "mean" on the whiteboard. "That's possible. But what if I told you the reason we're setting bedtime at 10:30 is so we can all get up in time to have a weekend adventure? Your dad and I have decided that we want to start using weekends for fun family activities."

The boys gave each other surprised looks. "What kind of things?" Marcus continued, acting as the boys' spokesperson.

Kim wrote "Fun activities" and started a list on the whiteboard. She held up the marker. "Who wants to write down something they would like to do together as a family on weekends? Brent jumped up and took the marker. He wrote down: "Go-carts."

"Good job, Brent." Kim underlined "go-carts." She offered the marker again. "How about you, Marcus?" He grinned and jumped to the board. He looked at Kim and said, "Is this for real? Are you being serious?" Kim nodded and handed him the marker. He wrote down: "River rafting."

"Excellent idea, Marcus," Kim said. She turned to Aiden and extended her hand with the marker. Aiden took it and looked at everyone around the room. The mood had lifted considerably.

With a grin the size of Texas, Aiden wrote: "Drone-flying lessons."

John jumped up and gave Aiden an exuberant high five. "Now you're talking!" John took his turn at the whiteboard. "Okay, we have, "mean." Should we leave this on the list?"

"No!" the boys shouted in unison. John scrubbed the word. "Now look at this, boys. Go-carts! River rafting! Drone training! If we start this weekend, we have things to do every other weekend ahead for a while. Okay, everybody gather round and let's make a plan. We'll have to plan ahead for drone school and the same with rafting. Mom, will you make reservations for these two things?" Kim nodded, smiling. "Meanwhile, this weekend what do you guys say we drive go-carts? Boys, can you find us the best place with the fastest carts?"

"Yes!" the boys yelled.

John took the marker and went back to the whiteboard. He circled "10:30." He looked at each of the boys and at Kim and paused to build excitement. "Can anyone tell me what this is again?"

Marcus laughed and said: "That's our new weekend bedtime."

Kim rubbed his head. "Marcus, you really catch on fast!"

The kids talked energetically as Kim gave John a big kiss. "Thank you," she whispered in his ear.

John grinned and then held up his hand to quiet the room.

"Okay boys. You all need to thank Kim for coming up with this idea. The reason she wanted us to get our butts in bed on weekends is because she wants us to be having fun together. The earlier we get started, the more we can do." He let that sink in, then continued. "We can brainstorm more things as we go along. And I want you to keep something in mind. If you notice, all of these activities cost money. So, when you think of ideas, try to come up with things that are less expensive but still fun."

"Like hiking and exploring?" Aiden ventured.

"Exactly," John replied. He looked again at Kim and motioned her to take over.

"Alright. Does anyone want to go back to sleeping late on weekends?"

"No!" came the chorus.

"So when I say it's time, you guys agree to go to bed? And if you give me a hard time, do you know what will happen?"

Heads nodded all around. "Okay, then. Saturday is go-carts. You boys better start planning."

. . .

Meanwhile, Kim had been drafting a written agreement for everyone to sign specifying that Friday and Saturday bedtime would be 10:30. Every other weekend, the boys would earn a family activity to be planned by the group during a family meeting. Everyone happily signed and the document was placed safely in the family notebook where they stored their agreements.

## Resolving Conflicts

We are all influenced by our childhood experiences. Some swear they will never repeat their parents' mistakes; others follow, knowingly or not, in their parents' footsteps. Couples have to negotiate differences that have grown out of their separate experiences. They also have to deal with changes continuously taking place in the world. Standards of behavior have changed and even the definition of family has changed. Child-rearing practices have become more varied as well. We used to know what to do when families consisted mainly of two biological parents and their children; we could follow traditional approaches. But how do we determine best practices for parenting in today's world? Which theory of parenting should we follow? If you read parenting blogs and advice columns, someone has a new idea almost every day—most of them unproven. Is there a right way or a wrong way? Is there a proven theory?

When couples conflict over child-rearing methods, negative emotions disrupt rational thinking. Instead of a flow of information focused on solving a problem, people fall into an exchange of hostilities, and coercion rears its ugly head. Coercion erodes loving relationships at all levels within the family—parent to parent, parents to children, and children with each other. Conflict disrupts effective problem-solving. When problem-solving discussions end in fights, problems remain unresolved and resentments accumulate, creating an increasing level of chaos in the family.

Couples who learn to solve problems together are able to reduce future stress, increase positive parenting practices, improve the couple's relationship, and reduce children's behavior problems. Skillful couples can avoid being manipulated by each other or by their children by choosing the right time to talk, resolving disagreements privately, and presenting a united parenting front. Parents we work with learn to combine the skills described in previous chapters—particularly regulating emotions, active listening, and problem-solving—and adjust them for adult-to-adult interactions.

Now you can apply these skills to strengthen your own relationship. When you disagree with your partner on how to reach a shared goal, whatever the goal may be, we urge you to follow these strategies.

## Strategies for Resolving Conflicts

- Use good timing.
- Create a positive context for the conversation.
- Take turns as speaker and listener.
- As speaker, plan how to present your goal statement.
- As listener, pay careful attention.
- Regulate emotions.
- Be prepared to compromise.
- Seek a common goal.
- When you agree on a goal, write it down.
- Brainstorm.
- Consider the pros and cons of ideas.
- Design a plan.
- Try it out.
- Revise and try again.

Kim and John used all of these strategies during different phases of their problem-solving process. When they were alone together, they carefully listened to each other's perspective to reach a common understanding, and that facilitated compromise. When they engaged the boys in the discussion, the foundation for united decision-making had already been established. The parents got the boys' buy-in by engaging them in brainstorming to plan weekend activities. The importance of writing down these agreements cannot be underestimated. As parents, we forget the details of our promises. And children tend to hear only what they want to hear. A written document dignifies the agreement for everyone.

# Recap

Perspectives on the roles of mothers and fathers vary enormously, and the differences are often the cause of conflict between partners. But *vive la différence*! Not only is it okay to disagree; contrasting viewpoints can expand the range of options. Be aware that children often contribute to the problems by fanning the flames of conflict—sometimes inadvertently and sometimes not so accidentally. Be strategic in choosing a time to talk about difficult issues. If either person is in a bad mood, this is not the time to talk about problems. If your discussion leads to conflict, disengage and make a date to talk another time. Solving problems works best when people are in good moods and have plenty of time, not when they are rushed, hungry, or upset, and especially not when one or both of you have been drinking.

Create a pleasant environment for your discussion, a place with few distractions that is conducive to positive interaction. Open the discussion by talking about something you both enjoy, or a successful experience one of your children had, or a recent pleasant event. Once you have established a favorable context, you can begin your problem-solving session. For Kim and John, camping without the boys became their favorite way to resolve family issues. Even if you can't stay together as a couple, you *can* present a united parenting front.

## Practice Assignment

☑ Make a list of two or three topics about which you and your partner (or a friend or family member) disagree or have differing points of view. Order them according to the intensity of the disagreement. Select the *least* hot topic for your first conversation. Discuss only one topic per session.

☑ Make a date to hold the discussion. Go out together as a couple. If you are having the discussion with an adult family member or a friend, make a date for the meeting as well.

You don't have to have a weekend camping trip, but do find a time and place that you both enjoy. Plan ahead to discuss the issue and set a goal to make progress, even if you don't entirely resolve the issue.

☑ Follow the strategies for managing conflicts given below.

## Strategies for Managing Conflicts

🖐 *Disengage.* Remove yourself from emotionally hot situations and calm down.

🖐 *Define your goal.* Be specific and future-oriented. State what you want. Talking about the past can provoke negative reactions and prevent forward movement.

🖐 *Write down your goal.* Keep it with you and restate it when the conversation gets off topic.

🖐 *Listen in a sensitive or caring way.* Use active listening skills. Show that you understand the other person's point of view. Be soothing. Don't fan the flames of conflict.

🖐 *Plan ahead.* Develop a good plan of action. Gather information. Search for new ideas.

🖐 *Consult with others.* Ask friends, family, or professionals to help sharpen goals and action plans.

🖐 *Use good timing.* Talk when people are in a good mood and there is enough time. Don't bring up problems when people are rushed, hungry, upset, or have been drinking.

🖐 *Choose your place.* Should the setting be public or private? Quiet or noisy?

- *Plan your presentation.* Think of different ways to introduce the subject. Be tactful. Don't just say the first thing that comes to mind.

- *Rehearse your presentation.* Practice out loud so you can improve your tone of voice. Use the mirror to correct your facial expressions and body language.

- *Anticipate reactions.* Imagine the discussion. Prepare for the best and worst possible scenarios.

- *Rehearse your response to anticipated reactions.* Ask a friend to role play the other person in the conflict. Try out different reactions and responses.

- *Acknowledge your own responsibility.* If you admit to a share of the blame, the other person may be more cooperative.

- *Be prepared to compromise.* Both sides may have to give a little.

- *Design a plan.* Write out an agreement.

- *Revise plans.* Difficult or enduring problems don't change with the first try. After a fair test, improve the agreement.

# Chapter Eleven

# We Are Family

A s you can see, there's no magic here. All that we have is a set of strategies for changing families that you can adjust to meet your individual needs and those of your children's personalities and development. These flexible, commonsense strategies can help you to shape the family experience you're seeking. The hard work you've invested in being the best parent you can be and your continuing commitment to the long journey ahead are sure to pay off in a happier and more harmonious family life.

Let's quickly review the key principles we've covered so you can use them to their best advantage.

## Identify Strengths, Values, and Goals

In the first chapter, we asked you to make a list of your strengths and a wish list of hopes and dreams—goals for your family life. We talked about values. Values are solid and few people change theirs as a result of reading a book. By now, you may have a better image of the strengths of your family and everyone in it. For many of us, recognizing and celebrating strengths in ourselves and the people we love are skills that have to be developed and practiced. Another expertise you may have sharpened as you applied the strategies in this book is specifying goals—both long-term goals and the tiny steps required to reach them. Goal-setting puts you in charge of determining your life's course.

## Give Clear Directions

We have yet to meet a family that didn't love the basic strategy of: "(Name), do (behavior) now, please," followed by the stand-and-hold technique. It almost never fails to achieve your goal. My grandson is a cooperative child, but when he's playing a video game and it's time for dinner, I *must* follow the clear-direction strategy to the letter. I come up behind him, put my hand on his shoulder, make eye contact, and gently say: "Finn, it's time to come to dinner now, please." And if I forget and don't stand and hold, I have to go back and use the strategy exactly right the next time. It also helps to give him a five-minute advance warning. He says the warning helps him reach a good stopping point.

## Teach Through Encouragement

This is the parenting tool that children tend to like the most. They say that they feel appreciated when their parents notice their efforts to cooperate. Both parents and children tell us that the structure of an incentive chart helps them remember exactly what is expected. Token systems and point charts do away with the need to nag, and children develop a sense of mastery and self-confidence from doing a good job and being acknowledged for it. As your children fall into routines for carrying out each day's expectations and chores, you won't have to rely on this structure. The routine is learned and becomes a habit. But whenever you hit a bump in the road and need to help your children develop a new habit or learn a hard-to-master skill, it may be time to reinstate the structure of an incentive chart. Remember not to require perfection—70 percent is a reasonable goal. Encourage any steps in the right direction And give daily rewards to reinforce the desired behavior and bring out the smiles.

# Identify and Regulate Emotions

I remember when I first studied emotions, learning their indicators and strategies for regulating them. I felt as if scales had fallen from my eyes. I used to think that I understood emotional undertones, but I was never confident in my beliefs. As I began to recognize that some signs indicate anger, others anxiety, and others sadness, I became more compassionate, especially when I learned that my emotions often elicited entirely different reactions in my kids.

There are those who believe that it's good policy to "let it all hang out." We do not. They tell you that it's harmful to suppress emotions and that negative emotions are part of living, part of survival. Yes, but understanding them and controlling them enable us to use our emotions to create the changes we want or need. When you're angry, you have to re-center yourself so you can remember your problem-solving strategies. When you regulate your emotions, you help other family members regulate theirs. We are models for our children's behavior. We don't have to be victims of our emotions. We can direct them and shape them. And when we do, we contribute to a spirit of cooperation throughout the family.

# Set Limits

For most of us, the hardest part of parenting is using discipline effectively. Contrary to what many famous psychologists say, our randomized, controlled studies clearly show that parents must use negative consequences when their children misbehave, violate rules, or get into trouble. Our strategies for sanctions are mild, predictable, and designed to be delivered in a calm yet firm manner. Punishment, or limit-setting if you prefer to call it that, is not effective when that is the primary way you teach your children. You have to balance negative consequences for misbehavior carefully with encouragement for the behaviors you want to promote.

For some reason, problem behaviors attract our attention more than positive behaviors and we forget to shine the light on what we want to grow. It's true that you have to discourage those nasty weeds, but your garden will be barren if that's all you do. When you provide an environment rich in encouragement, you not only promote cooperation, you also have fewer weeds to pull. When you must use negative sanctions, keep consequences mild and immediate, and then let it go. It's over and in the past. You will feel better as a parent, and your children will accept their consequences more willingly.

## Listen—Really Listen

Most of us know that we're supposed to listen—really listen—to each other. But most of us are busy, in a hurry, distracted, or otherwise occupied. Then we don't give our children and our partners the attention they deserve. Active listening enables you to gain insight into your children's lives and share their worlds. Becoming a good listener also makes you a more caring and thoughtful person. Unfortunately, bad habits interfere with listening. For example, sometimes, hearing another person's story makes you want to tell your own tale, and then you are no longer listening. At other times, the story you hear may evoke all kinds of emotions, and you react rather than listening empathically. And then there are the times when you seize the opportunity to give advice rather than simply listen. When you feel as if you have an answer that will help, it's hard to save your expertise until your advice is requested. Remember to practice active listening and give your children the full attention they deserve. They will respond in kind.

## Resolve Problems Together

Life is full of difficulties, challenges, land mines, barriers, and conflicts that need resolution. The life you seek requires that *you* figure out how to make it happen, and that is when problem-solving skills come into play. The first step is to know what it is you want; then, you can design a plan to achieve it. A common mistake people make is to limit their options by going with the first idea that emerges.

Brainstorming *before* deciding on an approach broadens your field of options. Brainstorming as a family builds buy-in from all. When people work together to make plans, solve problems, and resolve conflicts, everyone has a stake in the solution. Our studies show that families who solve problems together are able to reduce future stress, enhance couples' parenting skills and relationships, reduce depression, and prevent and reduce children's behavior problems. Have you made family meetings part of your weekly family routine yet? If you have, you have probably discovered that your children enjoy them and benefit from contributing to the decision-making process. The collateral benefit is increased cooperation with agreements.

## Monitor Your Children

This set of skills involves keeping a watchful eye on your children's whereabouts, friends, and activities. Knowing these details enables you to keep them safe and on the right path. What is the right path? That's for you to decide, depending on your values and your children's interests and talents.

Parents often struggle with deciding how much oversight they should provide. You have to evaluate that based on your children's age, responsibility, and dependability. As children mature and spend increasing time away from home, you must consider several questions. Do your children go where they say they're going? Do they do what they say they're going to do? Do they come home on time? Do they hang out with responsible friends? If the answer is "yes" most of the time, you can relax. However, if your environment is dangerous or filled with seedy characters, increase your monitoring.

Many parents provide supervised time by engaging their children in skill-building activities like sports, lessons, and clubs. Working parents have to find appropriate and engaging daycare and after-school activities. Be sensitive to situations that make it hard for your kids to make good choices. Too much free time can lead to mischief. No free time can lead to overdependence. If you live in a safe neighborhood, you're lucky. If your children play with others who are well socialized and supervised, again you are lucky. When major transitions take place (moving to a new town or a new school, divorce or repartnering, natural catastrophes like flooding or fires, death or serious illness), children need guidance, structure, and support, and they may need your help with building peer relationships. Transitions are times of adjustment for parents, too, and sometimes we forget to notice how our children are adapting. Determining the proper amount of monitoring for each child is another balancing challenge for parents.

## Teach and Learn

One of the nice things about the educational process is that it is well structured. There is a curriculum for each grade, benchmarks are widely recognized, and grades are given that evaluate your children's performance. As parents, we are our children's best teachers and can help them through this process by providing structure at home as well. Incentive charts, homework routines, and checklists help both parents and children survive the many schooling challenges.

Another way that parents support their children's education is through regular communication with teachers. Some parents volunteer to help with school activities. Others talk with teachers when things are going well. Then, when problems arise, there is a solid relationship from which to work. Your involvement in school tells your children that you care about their education. It's another way to express your values with regard to a very important part of their development. Children spend the greater portion of their waking hours in school learning the skills required to survive in today's world and the social skills they need to get along with peers.

# Stand United

There is nothing quite as reinforcing as having a partner to help you figure out the complexities of raising children and dealing with life's everyday issues. Adults disagree with each other. That's a fact of life. We have different tastes, values, opinions, and interests. Our own experiences growing up taught us specific viewpoints and styles of living, which can clash as families live together in close quarters. Stress exacerbates these differences, and small disagreements can escalate into major conflicts, leaving room for coercion to rear its ugly head. That's why it's important to regulate emotions, listen to your partner's point of view, and use your best problem-solving skills. Disengage from disputes and wait until an appropriate time to make a plan. Play helps. And that's the final topic of this book—balancing work, play, and love.

# Work, Play, Love

Raising children is one of the most difficult jobs there is. Parents often feel as if they are on a merry-go-round, spinning through the days and weeks, dealing with one transition or crisis after another. Sometimes we feel overwhelmed by the demands of parenting and worried about our ability to create a safe and loving family environment. At these times, you have to press the reset button. Play is a good way to do this.

Having fun is a remedy for the stress and struggle of daily life. As we grow up, we learn to be responsible. But some adults become overly focused on fulfilling obligations and forget to make time and save energy for enjoyment. When we squeeze joy out of daily living, we rob, not only ourselves, but our families of opportunities for relaxation, stimulation, and creativity. For many, parenthood leads to overcommitment and the feeling of carrying too much responsibility. While work and commitment to family are important, don't forget to be kind to yourself or you may lose the resilience you need to bounce back from adversity. The combination of too much work and too little play destroys relationships and kills optimism.

Play is not just for children or retired people, or reserved for extended vacations. Play needs to extend to all levels within the family. We need time on our own—couple time, family time, and opportunities for family members to share positive experiences. The activities will vary depending on your values and preferences, and the ages and interests of your children. Some parents support their children's involvement in team sports. Other families spend time together playing cards or board games, reading books aloud, listening to music, or making music by singing or playing instruments. We love the outdoors, and so do our children. We spent time together as a couple and as a family skiing, fishing, backpacking, camping, sailing, and canoeing. Each of our kids seemed to like at least one of our activities, but none of them liked them all. Our wide set of options enabled us to spend time with each of our kids doing at least one thing they enjoyed. When families play together, children develop mastery in recreational skills and their self-esteem grows.

Make playtime with your children a daily activity, just as you make time for brain-training. Build it into your family routines. You may want to play before or after dinner, or before bedtime. You may find it a good way to eliminate some of the excess screen time children engage in today. Your positive involvement shows you are interested in your children and the things they like to do. It's a powerful way to deposit funds in your "goodwill" account, which will go a long way toward balancing those times when you have to be the disciplinarian. During playtime, give your children your undivided attention. Turn off your phone, messaging sources, email, and other disruptors. Use your active listening skills, asking questions that help your children share their lives with you. Let them lead the way in pretend adventures. Studies show that children want their parents to be involved in their lives—even when they act as if you are a pariah or the greatest embarrassment on earth.

As I was growing up, we spent a lot of time at a rustic cabin my folks had in the mountains—a place where, from my perspective as a tween and teen, there was nothing to do but hang out in nature. We didn't have TV or computers or telephone service. We played cards, went fishing, and read books, and I spent a lot of time on the lake in our battered aluminum canoe. Little did I know that, when I reached adulthood, whitewater wilderness canoeing would become my great passion. As kids, we learned that, when you know the rules and can follow them comfortably, you are free to use them creatively. We learned sportsmanship—how to lose gracefully, and how to win with grace.

Family play is important and etches wonderful pictures into your family memory bank. At the same time, do not shortchange yourself in adult play. Adult relationships must be nurtured—not occasionally, but regularly. Caring for children can be such a demanding task that we lose sight of the importance of nourishing our adult relationships. If you are in a relationship, be it newly minted or enduring, make time for each other as a couple. Make dates to go out together and have fun. Identify the ways you like to get away and reconnect with the one you love by doing the things you love to do. When your relationship is strong, you provide a solid foundation for your family.

Yes, work and family responsibilities are essential to life. But so is play. Parents who play together are better able to resolve the difficulties of parenting together and enhance the quality of family relationships. Now that your children are more cooperative, you may discover to your surprise that you have become more cooperative yourself as a parent and as a partner. With these skills in place, you can relax and, perhaps for the first time, live together, work together, and play together with a new and genuine spirit of cooperation.

# Recap

Your life is in *your* hands. All you have to do is to take the reins and use your best skills and tools. Work is important, and so is play. Too much work and stress lead to irritability, which invites coercive interchanges with the people you love. And coercion erodes love. So take your tonic, and build play into your lives. It is as important as work, and it will enhance a cooperative and loving spirit in your family.

The strategies are simple and the rewards are great. Build on your own strengths and those of your children. Use incentives to teach new behaviors and support good habits. Catch good behavior early and often. Be consistent in your use of discipline. Keep it short, mild, and appropriate. Hold regular family meetings. Use problem-solving strategies to design the life you want. And most of all, remember to be good to yourself and to make pleasure an important part of your life. Your family will thank you for it.

# Strategies and Resources for Raising Cooperative Kids

## Chapter 1: Imagine

Strategies for Successful Goal Statements
Identifying Strengths

## Chapter 2: Follow My Directions

Basic Strategies for Giving Clear Directions
Enhanced Strategies for Giving Clear Directions
Tracking Sheet for Giving Clear Directions

## Chapter 3: Accentuate the Positive

Strategies for Teaching Through Encouragement
Strategies for Choosing Tokens
Explaining a Token System
Sample Token Behaviors
Strategies for Creating Incentive Charts
Success Grows with Small Steps—Bedtime Routine
Social Reinforcers
Tangible Incentives
Setting Up an Incentive Chart

## Chapter 6: Stop, Look, Listen

Strategies for Active Listening
Active Listening Don'ts

## Chapter 7: We Can Work It Out

Strategies for Problem-Solving
Strategies for Family Meetings
Ground Rules for Family Meetings
Problem-Solving Worksheet

## Chapter 8: Someone to Watch Over Me

Warning Signs for Caregivers
Guide for Babysitters

## Chapter 9: Teach Your Children Well

Ava's Incentive Chart
Benito's Incentive Chart
Strategies for Brain Training
Strategies for Power Reading
Student Study Skills Checklist
Parent Study Skills Checklist
Steps to School Success
Do I Know?

## Chapter 10: United We Stand

Strategies for Resolving Conflicts
Strategies for Managing Conflicts

# Acknowledgments

---

Because this book is based on decades of research, we have many groups to thank. Foremost we thank the thousands of families who have participated in our research and practice. Families have contributed by allowing us to observe them interacting in their daily activities in their homes, classrooms, playgrounds, and in conversations with each other and friends. They also described their experiences through interviews, focus groups, questionnaires, therapy sessions, and parent groups.

Our colleagues at OSLC and ISII have helped us gather information and develop procedures and materials to disseminate to parents and professionals in the United States and internationally. Grants from the National Institutes of Mental Health and Drug Abuse provided us with the resources to carry out our work.

Our own families gave us insight as we put into practice what we were preaching. Our children and grandchildren taught us what really worked and what needed to be changed as we faced the daily challenges of living together.

Finally, we thank our agents Jennifer Gates and Jane von Mehren, without whom this book would not have been published.

# About the Authors

©James Rexroad

Marion S. Forgatch, PhD, founder of Implementation Sciences International Inc., and senior scientist emerita at the Oregon Social Learning Center, is a frequent speaker at professional conferences. Her awards include the Distinguished Contribution to Family Systems Research from the American Family Therapy Academy. She is coauthor with Dr. Patterson of *Parents and Adolescents Living Together*.

©James Rexroad

Gerald R. Patterson, PhD, founder of the Oregon Social Learning Center, is well known for his pioneering work in child and family psychology. His awards include the Distinguished Scientific Award from the American Psychological Association. He died in 2016.

©Kevin Eans

Tim Friend is an award winning journalist with two decades of experience as a national reporter covering science and medicine. He is the author of *Animal Talk: Breaking the Codes of Animal Language*

# To Our Readers

Conari Press, an imprint of Red Wheel/Weiser, publishes books on topics ranging from spirituality, personal growth, and relationships to women's issues, parenting, and social issues. Our mission is to publish quality books that will make a difference in people's lives—how we feel about ourselves and how we relate to one another. We value integrity, compassion, and receptivity, both in the books we publish and in the way we do business.

Our readers are our most important resource, and we appreciate your input, suggestions, and ideas about what you would like to see published.

Visit our website at *www.redwheelweiser.com* to learn about our upcoming books and free downloads, and be sure to go to *www.red-wheelweiser.com/newsletter* to sign up for newsletters and exclusive offers.

You can also contact us at *info@rwwbooks.com*.

Conari Press
an imprint of Red Wheel/Weiser, LLC
65 Parker Street, Suite 7
Newburyport, MA 01950

*www.redwheelweiser.com*